T0209187

The
SCALE
FACTOR

Lose Weight and Gain Control of Your Life

ERIK THERWANGER

BALBOA.
PRESS

A DIVISION OF HAY HOUSE

This book is a work of non-fiction. Unless otherwise noted, the author and the publisher make no explicit guarantees as to the accuracy of the information contained in this book and in some cases, names of people and places have been altered to protect their privacy.

Balboa Press books may be ordered through booksellers or by contacting:

Balboa Press
A Division of Hay House
1663 Liberty Drive
Bloomington, IN 47403
www.balboapress.com
1 (877) 407-4847

Because of the dynamic nature of the Internet, any web addresses or links contained in this book may have changed since publication and may no longer be valid. The views expressed in this work are solely those of the author and do not necessarily reflect the views of the publisher, and the publisher hereby disclaims any responsibility for them.

The author of this book does not dispense medical advice or prescribe the use of any technique as a form of treatment for physical, emotional, or medical problems without the advice of a physician, either directly or indirectly. The intent of the author is only to offer information of a general nature to help you in your quest for emotional and spiritual well-being. In the event you use any of the information in this book for yourself, which is your constitutional right, the author and the publisher assume no responsibility for your actions.

Print information available on the last page.

ISBN: 978-1-9822-1272-8 (sc)
ISBN: 978-1-9822-1274-2 (hc)
ISBN: 978-1-9822-1273-5 (e)

Library of Congress Control Number: 2018911926

Balboa Press rev. date: 11/28/2018

DEDICATION

This book is dedicated to everyone who dreads stepping onto their scale, and to those who have gained weight and lost self-esteem. To those who have put the needs of others above their own needs, at the cost of their own health and fitness. To those who have taken care of others and stopped taking care of themselves.

This book is dedicated to you — for making the commitment to regain control of your life, by accomplishing one of the most life-changing goals: losing weight. Your desire to transform your body, despite your challenges, has been my motivating "factor" for creating this book and making your "scale" a positive experience in your life.

I also want to thank my family. Your support allowed me to embark on my journey to lose weight, keep it off, and feel great again. Because of your encouragement, I was able to stay the course and accomplish much more in life than just losing weight.

CONTENTS

CONTENTS

LOSE WEIGHT AND GAIN CONTROL OF YOUR LIFE

E very day, millions of people receive horrible, depressing, and frustrating news. Cautiously looking down, they take a deep breath and stare at the numbers between their feet. They step off of their scales, then back on a few more times, to make sure it was working correctly. But the numbers are unchanged. What's the one common denominator these people share? The same look of disappointment.

- Wouldn't it be great if your scale stopped being the bearer of bad news?
- Is it possible for your scale to become a positive factor in your life?
- Could you actually look forward to stepping on your scale again?
- Can you lose the weight you need to?

Yes, it absolutely is possible to do all of these. **The SCALE Factor** will not only show you how to lose weight, it will show you how to keep it off. Losing weight is not easy. If it was, everyone would do it. But losing weight is simple. Unfortunately, most people try to lose weight by focusing only on their bodies. Wait a minute... isn't that the whole point? Accomplishing your weight-loss goal ends with your body, but it begins with your mind — your thoughts. What you feed your mind is equally as important as what you feed your body. In fact, how you exercise your mind is also as important as how you exercise your muscles. When you fail to harness the power of your thoughts, you fail to use the greatest weight-loss tool you have.

Let's take a quick look at the typical way that most people approach their weight-loss goals. As the year comes to a close, they think about the shape they are in, and decide to do something about their physical condition. They make the commitment to go into the New Year with a new body. With the best of intentions, a pen and paper in hand, they excitedly write down how much weight they want to lose. At that moment, they have completed one of the world's most common New Year's Resolutions — to lose weight. Millions of people set this life-changing resolution every year.

It is always exciting to envision the new body that will be taking shape during the coming year and thinking about how amazing you will feel. You can even start to picture how fantastic you will look, and how much better your clothes will fit. You know that your energy level, self-esteem, and passion for life will be at an all-time high. What a great resolution this is. It is too bad that most people will achieve nothing. Most of these eager folks wrote the same resolution last year and will probably write it again next year. Why do so many people fail to accomplish something that could be so life-changing? Quite simply, they start off wrong.

How you start a weight loss plan will ultimately dictate how you finish. I know this because I tried to lose weight many times — and failed. I continued to fail until I learned how to harness the power of my thoughts, then combine them with a simple meal plan and a basic exercise routine. **The SCALE Factor** will teach you how to start with the right thoughts and end with the body you desire.

Like many of you, I did not intend to gain extra weight and get out of shape. As my life began to head in a different direction, so did the meter on my scale. Unfortunately, it was pointing in the wrong direction. For most of my life, I had always been in great shape. I was an active child. I played soccer, basketball, baseball, and was on a swim team. Three weeks after turning eighteen, my active lifestyle took on a whole new meaning as I enlisted in the United States

Marine Corps. Boot camp was 90 days of intense training, packed with physical and mental challenges that kept me in peak shape.

As reveille blared across the base, four intense drill instructors woke us up each morning before sunrise. Their mission was to transform an undisciplined group of recruits, known as Platoon 1095, into United States Marines. By the time I graduated from boot camp and earned the title of U. S. Marine, I could run for miles, march for hours (with a full backpack and rifle), negotiate any obstacle course, and perform countless calisthenics, especially push-ups. Our transformation took 90 days.

You can accomplish great things in 90 days. Keep that timeframe in mind because we will be discussing it in greater detail later (Chapter 4).

I served in the Marine Corps for four years and was honorably discharged just after the first Gulf War ended. I was excited to begin my new civilian life and start college. I transitioned from camouflage trousers to blue jeans, and I enjoyed not having to wake up each morning before the sun was out. No longer required to get a haircut every week, or even shave each day, my hair grew over my ears, and I had a permanent 5 o'clock shadow.

There was no one around to tell me what to do anymore, and I had no orders to follow. But there were also no requirements about my appearance. I was no longer required to "fall out" and exercise with my platoon or qualify for my Physical Fitness Test (PFT). I alone, was responsible for keeping myself in shape.

At first, it was easy to maintain my "Marine" physique. I consistently went to the gym, and I even became a certified fitness trainer with the YMCA for a short period. I really enjoyed training my clients and helping them get into the physical shape for which they were striving. I always asked them what their physical fitness goals were, and as you may have guessed, most of them had the same one: to lose weight.

I worked with people who ranged from being slightly out of shape to those who were extremely out of shape. Being in excellent condition, I could never figure out why so many people stopped taking care of themselves. It made no sense to me. Exercising gives you more energy, keeps your mind sharp, and acts as an amazing stress-reliever. Why would people let themselves go?

After graduating from Orange Coast College, in Costa Mesa, California, I was accepted to the University of Southern California. I had been attending USC for about one year when I met the woman of my dreams. Gina was filled with an excitement and enthusiasm about life that was contagious. We met at a restaurant and went on our first date the next night. That was November 17, 1995, and three years later, we would tie the knot.

Ten months after our wedding, Gina threw me an amazing surprise party for my "Big 3-0." With family and friends, we celebrated into the night without a worry in the world. I was happily married, in the best shape of my life, and my career in the entertainment industry was going strong. Life was great.

I was at work the next day, when Gina received a phone call that would change everything in our lives. She had been diagnosed with cancer: Non-Hodgkin's Lymphoma. We were told that it was very aggressive, and they would need to start her chemotherapy treatments right away. She was only twenty-seven.

Things moved from fast to out-of-control and we found ourselves focused primarily on Gina's survival. She was quickly scheduled for her first "chemo" session and I was given a crash course on being her caregiver. Becoming violently ill was just one of the many side effects from the chemotherapy treatments.

She required constant care to make it through her treatments. To easily administer the chemotherapy, her doctors inserted a Hickman

Line into her chest, with part of it extending from her body. Each night, I would clean the exit wound and flush the tube with saline. I also gave her two shots in her legs each day to boost her immune system. As her caregiver, I was not only focused on taking care of her, but I was trying to keep our household running smoothly. I tried to maintain some sense of normalcy.

Gina was unable to continue working and was placed on disability as I struggled to keep up with both my job and my duties as her caregiver. I knew that I would need to leave my career in the entertainment industry and pursue a job that would allow me to have more control of my schedule and earn enough money to support us. But my options were limited.

I eventually found an opportunity in the financial services industry. After passing a series of tests, I was licensed to sell. Of course, I knew very little about financial products and even less about sales. We were experiencing so many challenges, so rapidly, that it was often tough to keep up with them all. Cancer dramatically shook the foundation of our lives. In addition to the drastic effects from her treatments, we started to feel the pinch from our financial struggles.

Over the next few months, Gina's condition worsened. As she continued to fight for her life, I continued to fight to earn a living. Our lives did not remotely resemble the lives we had just one year earlier as we walked down the aisle together. The chemotherapy caused Gina to become ill at the slightest smell of food, so I stopped cooking meals in our small, 860 square-foot apartment.

Based on my crazy "sales" schedule, I found myself eating on-the-run and grabbing a quick meal wherever I could, usually fast food. It was quick, inexpensive, and kept the smell of food away from Gina. I was eating later and later in the evening, and exercising had become a thing of the past. Life was moving so fast that I never realized just how out-of-shape I was becoming. I remember the first time I noticed my weight gain — it is still crystal clear to me.

My mom had stopped by to visit and she brought some pictures that she had recently taken. As I flipped through the photos, one caught my attention. It was a picture of my mom, standing with a guy who slightly resembled me, but this guy was a bit chubby.

I stared at the picture, realizing how much my physique had changed and how out-of-shape I had become. I still thought of myself as a Marine, but my body would never pass inspection. Many months of neglect had taken a toll on my health and appearance. Unhappy thoughts raced through my head. No matter what excuses I thought of, it did not change one fact: that guy was me. I had gained over 40 pounds, in just over a year. I could never understand how people could let themselves go... until I had let myself go.

I went into my bedroom and gazed into the mirror. I did not like what I saw. What had happened to me? Where was the Erik I knew? Where was the athletic, energetic, full-of-life person I used to be? I stepped on my scale and did not like the results I saw. Everyone handles their own weight gain differently, but for me, tipping the scale at 216 pounds made me feel embarrassed, disappointed, a bit angry, and thoroughly discouraged.

As a caregiver, I had made the commitment to take care of Gina and our household, but I stopped taking care of myself. Being overweight drastically affected my self-esteem. I was less confident, felt less attractive, and was becoming depressed. I did not feel like I was in control of my life. It is tough to perform at your best when you feel like you are at your worst.

Like many people, I set a New Year's resolution to lose weight. I started off strong for a few days. But within two weeks, I was back to square one. I tried, unsuccessfully, to restart my weight-loss plans, but continued to fail. I tried different diets and exercise routines, but I could not get them to click. I knew that specific factors led to my weight gain, and it would be my ability to control these factors that would lead to my weight loss.

By identifying and controlling three important factors, I not only accomplished my weight loss goal, but I exceeded it. I shed 42 pounds in 90 days. I succeeded with my weight loss goal by controlling three factors:

1. My thoughts
2. My menu
3. My body

How would you feel if you could shed your unwanted pounds in the next 90 days? Let me tell you how you would feel. GREAT! Too many people set the goal of losing weight, but never experience the joy of accomplishing it. In 90 days, you will lose weight and achieve a better body by applying the techniques in this book.

The SCALE Factor helped me to discover a new life, without starving myself, or killing myself at the gym. It combines the training principles I learned in the Marine Corps, my experiences as a fitness coach, and my unique goal-setting strategies.

The SCALE Factor will move you from the excitement of writing down your weight loss goal, to the true joy of seeing your accomplished goal in the mirror and on the scale. By following this simple plan for 90 days, you can lose weight, feel better, look better, and improve countless areas of your life.

Losing weight has helped me to accomplish other goals that have enhanced my life - personally and professionally. Accomplishing your weight loss goal can have the same impact in your life. When you take control of those three important factors: your thoughts, your menu, and your body - you take control of your life. These three factors got you into the shape you are in now and they will be the same three factors that will get you back into shape, starting today.

I lost the weight, kept it off, and enhanced my life. I am confident that you can do it too, and perhaps, inspire others to do the same. **The SCALE Factor** is my account of how I lost a life-changing amount of weight in a 90-day period. I wrote this book for one reason - to inspire you to achieve the life you desire.

Think GREAT,

Erik

FACTOR 1 - YOUR THOUGHTS

> "A man is but a product of his thoughts. What he thinks, he becomes."
>
> — Mahatma Gandhi

I have never met anyone who needed help to gain weight. But taking off those unwanted pounds, however, is a different story. Most of us do need some assistance. When I am asked to help someone with the life-changing goal of losing weight, it is one of the single greatest compliments that I can receive. I do not take it lightly. I love watching people achieve a greater life by shedding the dreaded pounds that weigh them down — in so many ways.

Gaining weight is a heavy toll on your mind, not just your body. I remember the horrible thoughts that filled my head every time I stepped onto my scale; every time I looked into the mirror. Some days, even after eating properly, I thought I would get a much better readout on my scale. But the number staring back at me often stayed around the same range. If I ate well for a week, I might lose a pound or two. But when I splurged a bit, I was guaranteed to put on three or four pounds. I never liked the way that math worked.

I had put on a great deal of weight with virtually no thought. Well, that was actually one of the factors that led to my problem; I had stopped thinking about it. When you are not focused on staying in shape, your physique can easily get out of shape. Your body follows your thoughts. Weight gain begins, not when your body stops working, but when your mind stops working. As I found out, life is filled with circumstances that can easily hinder your ability to stay fit. Factor 1: it is imperative to your weight loss goal that you stay in control of your thoughts.

As a personal trainer, I was always excited to work closely with my clients. I enjoyed putting together menu options and exercise routines to help them look and feel better. But one thing always troubled me. Although the people I trained became more physically fit, they often stopped their programs and returned to their previous habits. As their bad habits returned, so did their weight. Sometimes they gained more weight than they had originally lost. Their diet and exercises were working, yet they stopped. It didn't make any sense.

People often sabotage their goal of losing weight, even when their efforts have put them on track. I used to ask myself, "Why?" But I would not discover the true answer to this question until my life became filled with challenges and I became someone who stopped focusing my thoughts on my own fitness goals.

RIDING A TRICYCLE

Trying to lose weight by only dieting and exercising is like trying to ride a tricycle without the front wheel. Sure, you can get a little momentum going, but the ride will be short-lived. As you continue to crash your tricycle, you eventually become frustrated and ultimately give up. If you fall enough, you may even stop trying.

But what if you had that front wheel, and you could control it? How far could you go? I bet you could make it all the way to your weight loss goal, and perhaps further. That front wheel is vital because it provides your journey with balance and guidance. Your front wheel is the first factor in your weight loss goal: your thoughts. It is the most crucial component to losing weight, yet it is frequently the most underused.

People fail to lose weight because they fail to control their thoughts. Once I harnessed the power of my thoughts, the "menu" and "body" wheels rolled a lot smoother on my tricycle. Yes, losing weight is like riding a tricycle; once you learn how to do it properly (using all three wheels), you never forget. That is how I lost my excess weight, kept it off, and now teach others to do the same.

Tapping into the power of your thoughts will allow you to stay on course with your weight-loss goal, even when faced with challenging circumstances. Tough times always create some pretty convincing reasons for not pursuing your weight-loss goal, even if you have already gained momentum. I know because I had some very convincing excuses: Gina's cancer, my new career, and financial troubles topped my list.

Neither my eating habits nor my exercise routine helped me to stay on track with my goal during tough times. But my ability to control my thoughts allowed me to stay the course until I stepped back on my scale and saw my desired numbers. **The SCALE Factor** is unlike any other weight-loss book. It focuses on empowering the one person who can guarantee that you will accomplish your weight loss goal. You!

You will change your way of thinking and start identifying the strong reasons you have for losing weight and getting back into shape. This book is not meant as a quick fix, but rather a life-changing journey to better health and a greater life.

Divided into three powerful sections, **The SCALE Factor** pays careful attention to the factors necessary to reach your desired results.

> **Factor I: Your Thoughts** — Uncovers the **Psychology of Weight Loss**, unlocks the power of your weight-loss

goal, unveils the five steps to accomplishing that goal, and explains the power of a 90-Day Run to help you stay on track.

Factor II: Your Menu: — Identifies the "growing" problem of weight-loss, points out why there are no "quick-fix" solutions, provides you with a nutritional education, supplies recipes for easy-to-make healthy meals, and teaches you how to effectively schedule your meals.

Factor III – Your Body - Shows you the many benefits of physical activity, with an emphasis on a simple, time-efficient program that includes stretching, a cardiovascular program, and a weight-training routine.

The SCALE Factor is a simple approach to weight loss that will not only fit into your schedule but will provide you with more time and energy to pursue your other goals. Losing weight is not always easy, but it can be as simple as riding a tricycle. If I could lose 42 pounds in 90 days, so can you. Life is better when you start to lose weight. You will have more energy, more excitement, more drive. You will soon find that your other goals will become more attainable.

While your eating habits and exercise routine are important, your thoughts will be the foundation of your weight-loss goal. As you develop a strong mental foundation, you can successfully add a meal plan and exercise plan to your life that you will, once and for all, stay committed to.

By losing weight, I improved both my personal and professional life. Over the next 90 days, as you apply **The SCALE Factor**, you will increase your ability to accomplish one of the most life-changing goals: losing weight.

The first step is for you to make the choice to lose weight. Break out your pen and answer the following question with a big, confident YES or NO!

Are you ready to lose weight in 90 days?   YES _____   NO _____

THE PSYCHOLOGY OF WEIGHT LOSS

Your Mind is Your Greatest Weight Loss Tool

The fitness goal I encounter the most is simple: weight loss. People usually are not striving to be bodybuilders, to have 6 pack abs, or to be featured on the cover of the next fitness magazine. Those are great goals for some, but most people just want to regain control of their bodies, and thus, their lives. They want to release the anchor "weighing" them down.

According to consumer market research firm, NPD Group, "62% of adults and 34% of children are overweight or obese, a percentage that has been virtually the same since 2001." The sad part is that nearly every person who has been overweight, or currently is, has tried unsuccessfully to remove those pounds. Understandably so, most people focus on diets and exercise to lose weight.

Eating healthy foods and exercising properly are essential steps, but most people revert to the patterns and habits to which they are conditioned. Adopting new patterns and habits are important to lose weight, but the old ones cannot merely be swept under the **SCALE**. To begin my weight-loss quest, I looked into the similarities that people share, especially those who have gained weight, and have had trouble losing it. As I identified their common denominators, I discovered the **Psychology of Weight Loss**.

Understanding this concept allowed me to have greater control over my thoughts, which ultimately helped to position me closer to my weight loss goal.

The **Psychology of Weight Loss** introduces two opposing factors:

1. Enemies of Weight Loss
2. Friends of Weight Loss

Most people struggle to lose weight because they only allow their thoughts to focus on their "friends." You know the old saying, "Keep your friends close and your enemies closer." So, let's take a closer look at the Enemies of Weight Loss — the negative factors that contributed to my personal weight gain.

THE ENEMIES OF WEIGHT LOSS

When I finally admitted to myself that I was overweight, I searched for the explanation of why I had let my body get out of control. Shortly after Gina was diagnosed with cancer, we started to experience additional financial hardships as a result of her being on disability and me switching to a sales career. As the pressures compounded in our lives, I dedicated much less time for planning my meals and virtually no time for exercise. My thoughts were consumed by other areas of my life and I paid the price with my physique.

The stress in our lives was a significant "enemy" to contend with, but it was not the only one. Two other enemies would work together to successfully direct my thoughts away from staying fit. The **Enemies of Weight Loss** have a significant impact on your ability to successfully lose weight. Being aware of them is the first step to taking control.

The Three Enemies of Weight Loss:

1. Conditioning

2. Stress
3. Lifestyle

ENEMY #1: CONDITIONING

Bad habits are hard to break, especially if you lack focus. From the time of our birth, we are taught how to eat, what to eat, and when to eat. For our first eighteen years of life, most of us are conditioned what to eat by adults, usually our parents. And in turn, our parents were conditioned by their parents.

Even with the best of intentions, many children are not taught healthy eating habits, including portion control. Parents are typically not nutrition experts, and much of our food now comes prepackaged and processed, which explains why there is such a problem with obesity today. Even the best personal trainers can experience great reluctance from their "weight-loss" clients because of this deep-rooted conditioning.

As adults, we took the eating habits we were conditioned to follow, then modified them to get to the point we are at right now. If you are 40 years old, you have about 18 years of conditioning from your parents, and another 22 years of your own. Never underestimate the power of conditioning. Your weight gain did not happen overnight, nor will you lose it overnight. But you can start breaking that old, unhealthy habit of poor conditioning right now.

Weight gain can happen in many ways as a result of our conditioning and the choices we make. Speaking to thousands of people about their own weight-loss goals made me realize that I was not the only one to be conditioned to gain weight.

Common Forms of Conditioning:

- Clearing Your Plate (portion control)

- Unhealthy Rewards (encouraging good behavior with bad foods)
- Preparing Unhealthy Meals (using processed foods or fast foods)

CLEARING YOUR PLATE

As a child, I remember staring at the remaining food on my plate, usually the vegetables. It seemed like an eternity for me to eat my broccoli, carrots, and peas. I actually felt full, but my parents instructed me to sit there "until you clear your plate." Sound familiar? Their intentions were good, but they were teaching me to eat everything that was in front of me, every time I ate, whether I was full or not.

My parents were raised in similar ways. Even though they both had gained weight, they did not see the correlation between too much food on their plate and being overweight. Many children are taught to clear their plates, so they do not waste food. This type of conditioning is powerful and can be a difficult habit to break. As these children become adults, many actually feel guilty about leaving food on their plates.

The American Institute for Cancer Research conducted a study and found that people tend to mindlessly eat what is on their plate, even if there was far more food than they actually intended to eat. The study revealed that people eat up to 56% more calories than they normally would, simply because the food is present.

The American Cancer Society has also linked diet and obesity to increasing the risk of certain types of cancer.

 Tip of the SCALE

To eliminate the feeling of guilt, plan your meals and your portions. Put less food on your plate and start listening to your stomach. Train yourself to stop eating before you feel full. There is nothing wrong with leaving food on your plate, especially for healthy purposes.

UNHEALTHY REWARDS

Many child development professionals advise parents to reward good behavior, rather than disciplining bad behavior. The idea is that the child will start to focus on being "good" in order to be rewarded. Parents who favor rewards over punishments have experienced positive results. Unfortunately, many children, including myself, have received the wrong rewards, such as sweets and junk food.

How many times have children been given an unhealthy treat to take their minds off of a scrape on the knee? Or parents hand a snack to their children just to keep them quiet while the adults talk? Even as adults we tend to celebrate birthday parties, promotions, and our successes at our favorite "high-calorie" restaurants. More often than not, children grow up to be adults who perform good for bad food.

 Tip of the SCALE — Start to reward yourself and your children with items other than unhealthy foods.

PREPARING UNHEALTHY MEALS

One of the biggest contributors to weight gain is the planning and preparation of your meals, or should I say, the lack of it. Most people actually include healthy foods in their diet, but they have been conditioned to transform them into weight-gaining meals.

I remember helping one of my clients to lose weight. He gave me a breakdown of his current diet, and I was actually impressed with his choice of foods. His menu featured items like chicken, green beans, and a variety of fruit. Even the portions he initially described seemed reasonable, yet he could not understand why he was gaining weight. It wasn't until I discussed how he was preparing his meals that I discovered his true "enemy."

He started each day with breakfast, which is a healthy habit to follow. But his eggs were prepared as omelets, with cheese, and cooked heavily in butter. He admitted that he would often have a side of bacon or sausage, some hash browns, and sometimes a biscuit, with butter and jelly.

For lunch he would have a salad, but it would be soaked in dressing. Did you know that just two tablespoons of dressing can have up to 12 grams of fat and 130 calories? He didn't, and it was right on the bottle. He did eat a lot of fruit, but I noticed that he preferred the convenient canned fruit, in "heavy syrup."

For dinner, he enjoyed chicken, but it was often fried. He loved green beans, but only when they were mixed with mushroom soup to create a casserole. He was proud to let me know that he drank "diet" sodas with his meals.

Sadly enough, I understood his diet, because I was actually raised on a similar one. The more I thought about it, the more I realized that I prepared most of my meals the same way my parents did. That was a scary thought because my father died of adult on-set diabetes, which was directly related to his weight gain, and his diet. Unfortunately, he was unable to break the conditioning that was instilled in him for 60 years, and it cost him his life.

Tip of the SCALE Practice portion control by minimizing or eliminating the unhealthy items in your diet, such as salad dressing, sauces, and soda. Even tiny portions can add large amounts of weight, which are difficult to take off.

ENEMY #2: STRESS

Serving in the Marine Corps as an air traffic controller taught me how to handle a variety of challenges. I was comfortable in difficult situations and thought of myself as someone who always stayed cool under pressure. But Gina's battle with cancer, our financial troubles, and the challenges of my new sales career in the financial services industry were pushing me to the limit. I was under a great deal of stress. I did not let anyone know, but I felt the stress physically, mentally, and emotionally.

Stress is an enemy that has many negative effects. Our bodies have defense mechanisms that help us to adapt to difficult circumstances. When we encounter stress for prolonged periods of time, our bodies release a hormone called cortisol, which has many benefits. It helps our glucose metabolism, regulates our blood pressure, and assists our immune system.

Small amounts of cortisol are good and can help us to deal with stress by:

- Increasing levels of energy
- Decreasing sensitivity to pain
- Heightening memory functions
- Maintaining homeostasis in the body (stability)

But too much of anything, even a good thing, can be bad. Cortisol is no different and elevated levels of it can have negative effects on our bodies: blood sugar imbalance, high blood pressure, lowered immunity, and decreased thyroid function. Cortisol also plays a role in gaining weight. Having too much cortisol in our blood has another side effect — it increases our appetite.

How ironic; not only do you feel stressed-out, but your body's own defense mechanism will encourage you to eat more. That is exactly what had happened to me. After a stressful day, which happened most days, I came home and tried to relax on the couch. I would turn on the TV and grab something to eat, usually some form of "comfort food." Cupcakes, ice cream, and popcorn were my personal favorites.

I was bothered that I fell into the category of someone eating comfort foods. I was aware that these foods were not good for me, but I ate them anyway. These tasty snacks always made me feel better, at least for a short period. Like many people, I enjoyed my "unwinding" time later in the evening, which made it easier for my Enemies of Weight Loss to work together.

Going to bed with a belly full of unhealthy foods further compounded my own weight-gain problem. Looking back, these "comfort foods" never made me feel comfortable. I was uncomfortable in my clothes, uncomfortable looking at my reflection in the mirror, uncomfortable in front of others, and uncomfortable standing on my scale.

In today's high-stress culture, many people suffer from too much cortisol production in their bodies. Typically, people who have higher levels of cortisol tend to crave foods high in carbohydrates rather than those who function on lower levels of cortisol.

But here's the truly ironic part of this entire vicious cycle. Many people eat to deal with the stress of being overweight, which causes more weight gain, which causes more stress, which creates more cortisol, which makes them hungrier, which... well, you get the picture. Stress is one tough enemy.

 **Tip of the SCALE** Identify stressors in your life and take steps to alleviate them. Try replacing unhealthy foods with healthy alternatives. Exercise is a GREAT stress-reliever. (Part III).

ENEMY #3: LIFESTYLE

The way you live your life has a direct impact on how well you are living. It is estimated that over half of all Americans lead a sedentary lifestyle today; a lifestyle without physical exercise. The days of working on a farm or in a factory are all but gone. That was a time when people led much more active lifestyles and staying in shape was a side effect of their job descriptions.

Now, physical jobs have been replaced by desk jobs, which seldom require much more than typing on a keyboard. Activity during a normal work day may be nothing more than going for a walk — to the vending machine. Even children are feeling the effects of leading a less-active lifestyle. Many kids stay indoors and play video games, rather than participating in outdoor activities. The consequences of leading a sedentary lifestyle are immense: fatigue, mood disorders, heart disease, and the increased risk for cancer, just to name a few.

Perhaps the most common effect of this lifestyle is exactly what you were thinking: weight gain. Changing my lifestyle was a major factor in my weight loss. Sitting in front of the television typically tempted me to eat snacks. Most people do not change their lifestyle, unless something drastic happens. That is what happened in my father's case. After his eating habits brought on his diabetes, he slipped into a coma for three weeks.

When he came to, he was scared and very open to the suggestions of his doctor, one of which was to lose a significant amount of weight. My father lost more than 70 pounds and kept the weight off for a while. But eventually, he reverted to his old lifestyle — his bad patterns and habits.

The Enemies of Weight Loss worked against him and he passed away because of complications with diabetes. My dad was an amazing man, but this was one area that I did not want to be like him. I made the decision to lead a healthy, active lifestyle by making the decision to lose weight.

Tip of the
SCALE

Replace inactive leisure time, such as watching television, with active leisure time, such as taking a walk.

I am living proof that the three Enemies of Weight Loss (conditioning, stress, and lifestyle) work together to inhibit weight loss. Identifying these enemies showed me what I needed to "stop" doing in order to stay in control of my thoughts and stay on track to lose weight. I realized that they could only work against me if I let them. Being aware of them gave me the edge I needed.

THE FRIENDS OF WEIGHT LOSS

Stepping onto my scale and seeing the dial move farther and farther to the right made me feel terrible. My life felt like a train wreck and my body felt about the same. I lacked energy, enthusiasm, and drive. After identifying what I needed to STOP doing, it was time to take a closer look at what I needed to START doing. I began to combine the benefits of my "friends" — the factors that helped me to shed those unwanted pounds.

The Friends of Weight Loss:

- Thinking   -Your Thoughts
- Eating   -Your Menu
- Exercising   -Your Body

Most problems in life have simple solutions. I did not say easy, just simple. People who want to lose weight always want to lose it quickly. And that is one of the reasons they soon quit. Losing weight gradually and steadily is not only a healthier way to shed unwanted pounds, but also allows you to successfully keep them off. Take time and you will complete your journey and obtain your desired physique.

Losing weight and keeping it off requires a change in your thinking, not just making adjustments in your diet and exercise. It will take commitment and dedication, but if you are determined to lose weight, **The SCALE Factor** will teach you how to defeat the Enemies of Weight Loss, enlist the Friends of Weight Loss, and provide you a step-by-step guide to gain control of your life in 90 days

People are never surprised when I tell them that they need to change their eating habits and begin to exercise in order to lose weight. But they are surprised when I tell them that the first step is to change their thoughts. Controlling the way you are thinking will have the greatest impact on your weight-loss goal. Your mind is your most powerful tool when you are building a new body. Your mindset is more beneficial than any diet or exercise program, so let's focus on that first.

Now that you understand the **Psychology of Weight Loss**, let's get your thoughts linked into the power of your weight loss goal.

A MOTIVATING IMAGE

Bringing Your Big Picture Into Focus

I do not know how else to say it except, "I love goals." In fact, I love accomplishing goals so much, I wrote a book about it: *The GOAL Formula*. I love the feeling of empowerment I get from setting goals. I love the feeling of desire I get from striving toward my goals. And I absolutely love the amazing, life-changing feeling of accomplishing them.

But there is one thing I enjoy more. There is no greater feeling than helping others to accomplish their goals. It is one of my greatest rewards. As a goal coach, I have been able to help people to achieve greater results by sharing the concepts in my book with thousands of individuals, businesses, and organizations.

I teach people how to combine the elements needed to accomplish any goal, big or small, personal or professional. No matter what circumstances they face, I share the strategies necessary to realize their weight-loss goal.

When I first developed my formula, it did not take me long to realize that there is a big difference between a goal and a resolution. New Year's Resolutions tend to be made as a last-ditch effort to "resolve" a problem; a quick fix to a long-term issue. Resolutions are often vague and lack the deep emotional connection from the person who set them, which explains why most goals are never completed.

We are not going to let that happen with your weight loss goal. As you plug your weight-loss objectives into *The GOAL Formula*, you will immediately start to feel the excitement as you begin your journey to set and accomplish this life-changing goal. You will begin to visualize the new you. This formula will help to keep your thoughts focused on your desired physique, no matter what challenges you encounter.

As you transform your weight-loss resolution into an accomplished weight-loss goal, you will finish what millions of people only start every year. The remaining portion of this chapter is going to give you a thorough overview of my goal-setting process and show you how you can plug your weight-loss goal into this formula.

The GOAL Formula

Steps + Time + People =

Your Accomplished Weight-Loss Goal

THE POWER OF YOUR WEIGHT LOSS GOAL

What is the best part about a weight-loss goal? It's that you don't have to wait until your goal is fully accomplished to benefit from it. As soon as you start to apply the strategies in **The SCALE Factor** to your daily life, you will begin to experience greater results.

Your weight-loss goal is important for many reasons. Accomplishing it will help you to hit other goals you desire, and it will also open your mind (your thoughts) to new goals you may not have otherwise considered. Setting this goal gives you hope; accomplishing it gives you satisfaction.

Within the first two weeks of setting my weight-loss goal I not only started to see the results on my scale, but I started to feel better. I began looking forward to stepping on my scale. I experienced more energy and I started to feel reinvigorated about my life.

In addition to setting other goals, my confidence was continuing to grow. I felt empowered and it had only been two weeks. In fact, it was during this time that I came up with the idea of launching my company: Think GREAT.

Unwanted weight is like an anchor, constantly preventing you from sailing to new destinations. Those extra pounds you are carrying around are holding you back from the richness of your own life. Most importantly, they could be preventing you from realizing your **Big Picture** and achieving a greater life. What's a Big Picture, you ask?

YOUR BIG PICTURE

Have you ever tried to build a puzzle without looking at the box cover? We all look at the image on the front of the puzzle box. From the time we are children, we are taught to look at the completed image as we are putting the pieces together. Having a visual of the finished "picture" helps you to know what pieces to connect. Having your thoughts linked to your completed puzzle, your Big Picture, will help you to connect each of the pieces more effectively and more efficiently.

I accomplish the goals I set because I view each one as a unique piece of my puzzle — the Big Picture of my life. Developing and visualizing your Big Picture will help you to accomplish (and connect) all of the pieces necessary for you to have a greater life.

Goals are important, but they are only a piece of a more significant puzzle. My Big Picture is my greater purpose, my definition of a greater life. It is what I want out of life. It is the impact I want to make in my life, in the lives of others, and especially in the lives of those closest to me. My Big Picture is much "bigger" than any individual goal I have.

Accomplishing my goals is critical, as it moves me closer to achieving the life I desire. My weight-loss goal was no different, as it too, moved me closer to a more meaningful life. My Big Picture defines me. It motivates me, inspires me, and drives me. What defines you? What truly motivates, inspires, and drives you? What would empower you enough to make you not quit on your weight loss goal?

Let me share what my Big Picture was when I set my weight-loss goal. My daughter, Erika, was about one year old when I made the decision to get back into shape. What was different this time, compared to the other times I set out to lose weight? The difference was that I had pulled this goal from my Big Picture.

I was crystal clear about one specific part of my life. I wanted to be around to raise Erika. I wanted to live a healthy life and be here to watch her grow up. I wanted to be the best father she could have, and I did not want to die early, like my father did at age 60. With my eating and exercising habits, I was heading down the same unhealthy path my father did.

For obvious reasons, my weight loss goal became an essential puzzle piece in my Big Picture. Losing weight, to live a longer life, became a highly motivating factor for me; a factor that I would intensely track on my scale. Did the image of a greater life help me to accomplish my goal? Well, that day was the last time my scale ever read 216 pounds.

I was determined to accomplish my weight-loss goal because it would benefit my daughter, not just me. Most people set goals because of the benefit it will have in their life. But when you set goals because of the impact it will have in the life of someone important to you, your goals take on a greater purpose. When your goals are pulled from your Big

Picture, you will be virtually unstoppable. That is exactly how I felt during my quest to lose weight.

Do not just set a weight-loss goal, identify an important, life-changing goal that helps you to complete your Big Picture. If your greater purpose is important to you, it will keep you on track, especially during the times when life tries to throw you off track. Pulling your goals from this unique image will empower you as it did for me.

I tried to lose weight many times, but it wasn't until my goal was attached to my Big Picture that I not only accomplished it but exceeded it. The same can happen to you. Remember, every goal you set is a unique piece of an important puzzle in your life. It is up to you to connect the pieces.

Think about what is most important to you and who is most important to you. How will accomplishing your weight-loss goal help you to achieve a greater life? It may take you time to create your own unique Big Picture but starting to identify what is most important to you will produce a new level of commitment that will keep your thoughts focused on your weight-loss goal and will help you to stay the course.

A FORMULA FOR YOUR THOUGHTS

As a personal development coach, I discovered quickly that there is a difference between the way people set New Year's Resolutions and the way they set important goals. First, they wrote their resolutions down, which is always good. But things tend to go downhill from there. They often neglect to write a time frame for the completion of their resolution and seldom include the support of anyone they know.

Unfortunately, the piece of paper holding their life-changing resolutions gets tucked away, where no one can see. Now, you can transform your weight loss goal from a few words on a piece of paper to an unbreakable contract, connecting you and your Big Picture.

By combining the necessary elements for success and keeping your thoughts focused on your weight-loss goal, you will increase your chances for accomplishing it.

I remember when, and why I developed my book, *The GOAL Formula*. I saw firsthand the true power of having important goals and how essential it was to stay on track to accomplishing them. In August of 1999, I drove Gina to her first chemotherapy session. In the few days since her diagnosis of cancer we were both overwhelmed, scared, and searching for hope. This was about to be a very long journey.

Just before administering the potent chemicals into her body, her oncologist spoke to me privately. He told me it would be in Gina's best interest if I could "keep her spirits high." He told me it would help her to fight back against the disease and the harmful effects of the treatments. In other words, I needed to encourage Gina to keep her thoughts focused on nothing, but success.

His suggestion had nothing to do with her body but had everything to do with her mind. Keeping her spirits high was challenging, especially with the violent side effects of the chemotherapy. But I found that Gina responded most positively to setting goals; focusing on the things we would do when she was no longer sick. Buying our first home topped the list, so I focused heavily on that goal.

Accomplishing your goals, especially when life throws you a curve ball, is not easy. But it is achievable. By utilizing the power of *The GOAL Formula*, we purchased our first home and went on to set and accomplish many other goals, including financial, career, business, family, and fun goals. Your circumstances may not be perfect, but you can absolutely accomplish your weight-loss goal by using this formula.

The GOAL Formula combines three important elements:

1. Steps
2. Time
3. People

By taking the right **Steps**, in a specified block of **Time**, and enlisting the help of other **People**, you will increase the likelihood of accomplishing your weight-loss **Goal**. Together, we'll take these steps and develop your goal, in Chapter 3.

Make Your Goal a Reality

Accomplish More Than You Imagined

Most fitness programs, for obvious reasons, tend to focus mainly on the diet and exercise aspects of getting in shape. Although they briefly mention your weight-loss goal, they do not teach people how to successfully accomplish goals. They teach people how to diet and exercise, which is why so many constantly fail at accomplishing this life-changing goal.

Even those with a fitness trainer, helping them with their diet and exercise programs, often give up before accomplishing their goal. They eventually stop eating right and exercising, but they had stopped focusing on the weight-loss goal first. A "fitness" coach is good, but a "goal" coach is GREAT. That is what you now have with me.

I remember stepping off of my scale and making the decision to lose weight. I was determined to turn my weight-loss goal into a reality. My Big Picture was a powerful source of motivation and I was committed to losing weight and living a long, healthy life. I was focused on being around for my daughter and I was excited about what the next 90 days would bring.

I began to think about the new me, when I was looking and feeling better. I imagined how much better my clothes would fit and how much energy I would have in my day-to-day life. Just setting my weight loss goal gave me hope and inspiration. But it was time to plug it into my formula and make it a reality.

CHAPTER 3

When I first set my goal, I wanted to lose 16 pounds in 90 days. I was not trying to break any records, I just wanted to gain back control of my life. At that time, 16 pounds seemed like a lot to me. But getting my weight back down to 200 pounds seemed attainable in 90 days.

I plugged my weight-loss goal into the *The GOAL Formula*, applied the eating and exercising techniques in Part 2 and 3 of this book, and I did much more than accomplish my goal. I exceeded it. I dropped 42 pounds in 90 days. It is hard to put into words, just how GREAT it felt to lose that weight. In addition to surpassing my weight-loss goal, I started to accomplish other goals.

It all started when I plugged my life-changing weight-loss goal into a formula designed to transform goals into accomplishments. This chapter is dedicated to helping you to plug your goal into the same formula that worked for me.

Having a formula to lose weight allowed me to focus on my 90-Day Run, not on the challenges that could easily distract me. This allowed me to successfully implement a new eating and exercise plan into my life that would support my weight-loss goal. I stayed on track, ate healthy meals, and followed a basic exercise routine for 90 days. This all began when I started paying particular attention to my goal.

Now, it is your turn. You have attached your life-changing weight loss goal to your Big Picture and it is time to plug your goal into the same formula that helped me. Let's take a closer look at each element in this formula.

STEPS – THE 5 STEPS TO ACCOMPLISHING GOALS

Gina's diagnosis of cancer added a lot to our plate and our circumstances were less than ideal for setting and accomplishing goals. But it was imperative that I kept her spirits high. I searched for common denominators people used to hit their goals, so I could help Gina to accomplish hers. I found five distinct steps that empowered people to accomplish their goals, no matter what circumstances they faced.

I use the acronym G.R.E.A.T. to describe these five steps:

1. Goals   Identify important Goals in your life
2. Reasons   Establish powerful Reasons for accomplishing your goals
3. Expectations   Set high Expectations for yourself
4. Actions   Take all of the Actions necessary to achieve a greater life
5. Tracking   Intensely Track your results

Below is brief explanation of each step, followed by an example of how I used these steps to help reach (and exceed) my desired weight-loss goal. I have included a section, so you can write down each step as it relates to your personal weight-loss goal.

STEP 1: Identify Important Goals

Each person has a specific number of pounds they want to lose in order to accomplish their goal and experience a greater life. Some people have a substantial amount to lose, while others may only need to shed 10, 20, or 30 pounds to be back in shape. All weight loss goals take time, some more than others.

I divide goals into two categories: long-term and short-term. Long-term goals require more than 90 days to accomplish. These larger goals will be broken down into smaller, short-term goals you can accomplish them during a 90-Day Run. If your desired weight loss is 60 pounds, you could break that long-term goal into two short-term goals of 30 pounds each. By successfully completing two 90-Day Runs, and losing 30 pounds on each run, you will accomplish your long-term goal of losing 60 pounds.

The goal of losing weight holds different meanings to different people. You may want to shed excess fat, fit into your clothes better, improve your health, and/or boost your self-esteem, just to name a few. Accomplishing your weight-loss goal can mean the difference between having a life and truly living it.

Step 1 does not say to identify a goal, it says to **Identify Important Goals**. Important goals will create a stronger level of commitment and keep your thoughts focused in the right direction. Weight-loss goals can be life-changing, so yours must be **Important** to you. Create a sense of urgency for losing weight.

Writing down your weight-loss goal is essential. Trying to accomplish goals that are not written down is like building a house without blueprints. Your goal will develop a higher level of importance as you become more clear about your desired results. Just writing, "I want to lose weight" is never enough. You must be more specific.

Below is the initial weight loss goal that I set during my 90-Day Run. Write your goal below it. Include the exact amount of weight you want to lose. Describe the dress size or pant size you desire to fit in. Do you want to be healthier? Would you like to reduce your cholesterol or blood pressure? Perhaps you need to increase your energy and stamina. Make your goal important and write it down.

My Weight Loss Goal:
I want to *lose 16 pounds, fit back into a size 32 waist for my pants, and I want to have increased strength and energy.*

Your Weight Loss Goal:

STEP 2: Establish Powerful Reasons

A goal without a reason is like a car without an engine. Sure, it may look great, but it will take you nowhere. Just look at all of the amazing New Year's resolutions made every year. Those too, lack an engine. People get excited about writing out their resolutions for the New Year, but they typically throw in the towel within a couple of weeks. Why? Because they failed to write down their New Year's "Reasons."

People striving to lose weight will not get far by focusing only on "what" they want. Until they realize "why" they need to lose weight, they will continue to struggle with their weight-loss goal. Losing weight is a journey and your "why" paves your way.

Step 2 encourages you to **Establish Powerful Reasons** because the strength of your reasons will determine your success. When people attempt to accomplish weight-loss goals without powerful reasons to motivate them, they can easily get knocked off track. Have you ever noticed that whenever you attempt to accomplish something great, life has a unique way of putting obstacles in your path? Every time I have set goals, I have encountered some form of challenge in my life, sometimes numerous challenges.

There are reasons why some people are able to accomplish their weight-loss goals and others are not. Quite simply, it is the strength of their "reasons." My weight-loss goal was important to me. I knew that accomplishing it would not only change my life, but it would enhance the lives of those closest to me. As I thought about the importance of losing weight, I began to list out all of the reasons that compelled me to not give up.

The more I thought about my weight-loss goal, the more I thought about my family. It did not take me long to determine that my "why" was more important than my "what." I was no longer just trying to lose 16 pounds, I was determined to become healthier, so I could be around to see my children grow up. I wanted to grow old with Gina. I wanted to look like a Marine again (minus the haircut). I wanted to be in better physical shape, so I could perform better at my job.

I associated my weight loss to being able to provide a better lifestyle for my family and my reasons continued to flow. The more reasons I listed, the more confident I was that nothing was going to stop me. The daunting task of losing weight started to become much more achievable.

Below are the powerful reasons that I established for accomplishing my weight-loss goal. Write yours below them. Take time to think about "why" you want to lose weight. In addition to yourself, who else will benefit from the accomplishment of your goal? Will it be your children, spouse, other family members, or friends?

Establish your powerful reasons and write them down.

My Powerful Reasons for Accomplishing My Weight-Loss Goal:
I need to lose 16 pounds, so I will be healthier and live longer for my family. Losing weight will allow me to be a better father and husband. Losing weight will help me to look better, feel better, increase myself-confidence and have the stamina to pursue other life-changing goals that will benefit me and my loved ones.

Your Powerful Reasons for Accomplishing Your Weight-Loss Goal:

STEP 3: Set High Expectations

We all have basic expectations in our lives, such as showing up on time for work, dropping the kids off at school, and paying bills. Basic expectations will get you through life, but it will be your ability to elevate your expectations that will move you closer to the life you desire. I learned the importance of setting high expectations when I stepped off of the bus at the Marine Corps Recruiting Depot in San Diego, California in 1987.

Earning the title of United States Marine presented numerous physical and mental challenges for all of us raw recruits. In order to accomplish the important goal of becoming "one of the few and one of the proud," difficult tasks were constantly put before us. It would have been easy for any of us to give up, if it were not for the high expectations set by our drill instructors.

During that 90-day period, called boot camp, we would be learning new skills, taking new actions, and dramatically changing our patterns and habits. The expectations surrounding us matched the importance of our goal. Do your current expectations match the importance of your weight loss goal? To successfully lose weight during your 90-Day Run, you will learn new skills, take new actions, and dramatically change your patterns and habits.

Raising your expectations to match the importance of your goal will be paramount. Setting high expectations for yourself reinforces that your goals are important to you and will allow the right "productive" pressure to be applied to your weight-loss efforts. Elevating your expectations is like applying pressure to a lump of coal. Just the right amount will create a diamond.

Step 3 says to set high expectations, not low ones. Never set your expectations low because you might hit them. What would your life be like if you lived up to the high expectations you set for your 90-Day Run? It will be GREAT! Setting high expectations is one of the most effective ways of keeping your thoughts on your weight-loss goal.

My weight-loss goal was *important,* and my reasons were **powerful,** but it was my **high** expectations that would help me to stay in control of my thoughts and on track with my results. In addition to setting expectations about my eating habits and exercise routine, I also set a high expectation that was linked to my reasons, my goal, and my Big Picture. The main thing I want to encourage you to do is to not give up on yourself — do not quit.

Remember, millions of people desperately try to lose weight each year. Unfortunately, most of them never set high expectations for themselves and they give up before experiencing the benefits they deserve. Your weight-loss goal is too important for you not to set high expectations.

Take time to make an unwavering commitment to yourself. Set your expectations high and write them down.

My High Expectations for Accomplishing My Weight-Loss Goal:
I will control my thoughts. I commit to never quit, no matter what people say or how I feel. I commit to reviewing my goals, preparing healthy meals, and following my exercise routine. I will focus on the 3 Friends of Weight-Loss.

Your High Expectations for Accomplishing Your Weight-Loss Goal:

STEP 4: Take All of the Actions

There is a big difference between knowing what to do and actually doing it. Most people understand what they need to do to get in shape: exercise, eat healthier, stop smoking, minimize alcohol consumption, etc. But some people confuse movement with action. Putting on your exercise outfit and showing up to the gym does not translate into weight loss, but for many, that is as far as they get. You must use the equipment if you want to experience results.

There is an old adage that knowledge is power. If you are going to accomplish your weight-loss goal, you must combine knowledge with action. You need to take all of the actions necessary, not just some of them. **The SCALE Factor** provides information, and describes what actions to take, but it is up to you to do it. Taking action transforms your physical expectations into results.

I spent a great deal of time gathering the knowledge I needed to lose weight during my 90-Day Run. I took a close look at the valuable information I gained in boot camp and as a fitness trainer: daily schedules, nutritional requirements, and exercise routines. I needed to combine this knowledge with action, because I was not looking for a temporary fix. I needed a permanent change. My goal was to take off the weight and most importantly, to keep it off.

When you take the right actions, combined with the right knowledge, you immediately begin to enjoy the satisfaction of taking your life into your own hands. Although it takes time to see a physical change, taking action, especially when you do not feel like it, will produce results. I have often had the best workouts on the days I did not feel like going to the gym. Begin taking action, combined with the right knowledge, and start feeling better today.

Think about the actions that will bring you closer to your desired weight. Identify the necessary actions that you need to take and write them down.

My Necessary Actions for Accomplishing My Weight-Loss Goal: To lose weight, I will review my weight-loss goal and my results daily. I will eat healthy meals and eliminate junk food. I will follow a consistent exercise routine.

Your Necessary Actions for Accomplishing Your Weight-Loss Goal:

STEP 5: Intensely Track Your Results

Your weight loss goal is too important to just "wing-it." You have taken the first four steps: identified important goals, established powerful reasons, set high expectations, and started to take all of the necessary actions. The first four steps will help you to accomplish your goal, but only tracking will allow you to exceed it. By tracking my weight loss goal, I was able to turn my goal of losing 16 pounds into the life-changing reality of shedding 42 pounds.

No matter what important weight-loss goals you have identified, I am sure they have the potential to change your life. Whether you need to drop pounds, lose inches, or become healthier, you will need a tracking system to ensure that you are heading in the right direction and making any necessary course corrections along the way.

Tracking your progress helps to eliminate procrastination, allows you to course-correct, and causes you to become more accountable for your actions. Accountability, or lack of it, got you to where you are today, and it will also get you to where you want to be tomorrow.

Tracking is so important, but you never reap the full benefits when you try to do it alone. When you are accountable only to yourself it is easier to let things slide. This is the main reason I enlist the support of other people. When someone else is helping to track your results, it causes you to take more action.

I tracked my weight loss every morning on my scale. Just knowing I had to step on that thing each day made me less likely to cheat on my eating plan the night before. In addition to visually tracking my results on my scale, I reviewed my Eating Plan (Part 2) and Exercise Plan (Part 3) on a daily basis.

Below are the results I tracked intensely to accomplish my weight-loss goal. Write yours below them. Think about the results that will allow you to achieve your desired weight.

Decide which results you need to track intensely and write them down.

The Results I Need to Intensely Track to Accomplish My Weight-Loss Goal:

To lose weight, I will weigh in regulary and write down my results. I will review my eating plan and exercise plan daily.

The Results You Need to Intensely Track to Accomplish Your Weight-Loss Goal:

Congratulations! Not only have you plugged your weight-loss goal into *The GOAL Formula*, but you have already done more than most people do to stay on track with losing weight. Taking the 5 Steps to Accomplishing Goals allows you to begin the process of regaining control of your body and your life and do it permanently.

TIME MASTERY

Time is the second element in *The GOAL Formula*. The "lack" of time is one of the most common excuses I hear when someone tells me why they cannot lose weight. Time is a valuable commodity. Once it is gone, it is gone forever. You cannot lose weight yesterday and you will not succeed by putting it off until tomorrow. All you have is today.

Crazy, hectic schedules place a large demand on our time. The same schedules that allowed us to get out of shape in the first place, become obstacles for our new weight loss goals. It is essential to control your time and invest it in ways that support your weight-loss goal.

Your 90-Day Run will help you to utilize the same benefits I experienced in boot camp.

The benefits of a 90-Day Run:

- Patterns and Habits
- Rewards and Penalties
- Announcing Your Goals

There are significant benefits when setting up specified blocks of time to accomplish your weight-loss goal, especially in 90 days. By investing a small amount of time each day, you will become more productive for the rest of the day.

I utilized the benefits of a 90-Day Run to accomplish my weight-loss goal and I will show you how to do the same. We will set up your 90-Day Run in Chapter 4.

PEOPLE – ENLIST THE HELP OF OTHERS

Losing weight is a team effort and people often exclude others from their important goal. Many who write down their goals never show anyone that life-changing piece of paper. And casually mentioning your goals to others will not provide the desired response you need. Goals are more easily accomplished when you enlist the help of others. You can accomplish your weight-loss goal by yourself, but you will increase your chances of success by learning how to incorporate the support of others.

You may be thinking, "How is someone else going to help me to lose weight?" That's a great question. Having someone else eat the right foods for you does not help you to lose weight. And you will not get in shape by having another person exercise for you. But other people can provide your 90-Day Run with a very important component - accountability. I have found most people are better at holding others accountable, than holding themselves accountable. So, you can use that to your advantage with your weight-loss goal. You do not have to go at it alone.

When I set my weight-loss goal, I enlisted the help of my friend, Louis, to hold me accountable. I told him how much weight I wanted to lose each week and asked him to call me and ask me how I was doing. To make it more enticing, I gave him an envelope with $100 in it. I told him if I failed to stay on target with my eating, exercising, and weekly weight-loss goals, the envelope was his to keep, each week.

Guess who became very interested in holding me accountable? While Louis would have held me accountable for free, the $100 incentive added an extra level of focus (and fun) to my weight loss journey. I lost that envelope once, but I also lost those 42 pounds. Enlisting the help of others will greatly enhance your 90-Day Run. Here are some powerful ways that you can gain support from others:

- **Announce Your Goal** — Tell as many people as possible about your weight-loss goal. Tell them how much weight you will be losing and the time frames of your 90-Day Run.
- **Ask for Accountability** — Identify a few people who can regularly connect with you to check on your progress and review your results.
- **Choose a GREAT Partner** — As you announce your goals to your friends and family members, you may find someone with the same goal; the same desire to lose weight. They can go on a 90-Day Run with you.

I have always experienced greater results by enlisting the help of people in my personal network. Announcing your goals, asking for accountability, and choosing a GREAT Partner are all ways that will help you to stay on track to accomplishing the new you. Your weight loss goal is a personal journey that will yield amazing results. Break out of your comfort zone and share your life-changing goals with others. You may actually inspire someone to change their life as they witness the positive changes in yours.

YOUR 90-DAY RUN

Supporting Your Weight-Loss Goal

When it comes to losing weight, there are thousands of books, programs, and routines. Unfortunately, there are an equal number of excuses for not accomplishing this life-changing goal. I think I have heard them all. Do any of these sound familiar?

"I'm too old." "I'm too fat." "Working out is boring." "I don't like diets." "I don't have enough energy." "My back hurts." "My kids get in the way." "I don't have the right exercise equipment." And the most common excuse, "I don't have enough time."

Most people are uncomfortable with the lifestyle changes required to accomplish their weight-loss goals. They struggle to adopt new patterns and habits, even though these would provide them with a greater life. Their excuses help to rationalize their lack of action and tend to be more frequent when there is little to no structure to support their efforts.

When I started my journey from civilian to U.S. Marine, I knew it would not be easy. It was awkward, uncomfortable, and challenging. To accomplish the life-changing goal of becoming a Marine, I would need a system to support the activities required to develop the new me. Boot camp provided a 90-day support structure that allowed me to stay on track and complete my transformation.

Similarly, losing weight is not easy. It can be awkward, uncomfortable, and challenging. But the accomplishment of your goal will be life-changing. Like a raw recruit, you will need a system to support the

CHAPTER 4

activities required to develop the new you. Your 90-Day Run will provide you with the structure you need to stay on track and complete your transformation.

Structure is the missing element for so many people. Working a full-time job and being a parent can take up a considerable amount of time. School events, sports, social life, and family only add to the time constraints. People do not start programs, which can improve their lives, with the intention of failing. But unfortunately, most fail. Has this ever happened to you?

What happens when you add a life-threatening illness or other extreme challenge to the equation? Most people adjust their schedules and their weight-loss goals typically slide to the back burner. All too often I hear, "I will start it next week." But next week never arrives.

When it comes to accomplishing the goal of losing weight and keeping it off, remember this: it takes time. Your 90-Day Run will allow you to take control of your daily schedule and maximize the next 90 days. You will set up the time parameters necessary for successfully losing weight.

THE BENEFITS OF A 90-DAY RUN

One thing is for certain, the next 90 days are coming and there is nothing you can do to stop that. But there is something you can do. The big question is, what are you going to do with this block of time? How will you look on day 91?

The SCALE Factor will teach you how to use a 90-day block of time as a tool that will work to your advantage. You will be amazed at what you can accomplish during this time period. Are you ready to transform yourself into the person you know you can be?

Your 90-Day Run will provide the structure already proven to work. People have an amazing ability to accomplish much during this block of time. Many successful people and organizations implement some form of a 90-day or 12-week program to accomplish both their personal and their business goals.

The Marine Corps has used their 90-day program to transform over 1 million civilians into Marines. If it works for them, it can work for you. Boot camp was set up to completely support our goal of becoming a Marine. Outside distractions were cut off and we literally lived and trained in pursuit of our goal.

Real life is not like that. More than likely, you will have distractions, interruptions, and other obstacles in your path. During your 90-Day Run, you will be able to use many of the strategies and techniques that we used in boot camp — without having to enlist.

The Benefits of a 90-Day Run:

- Creating new patterns and eliminating old habits
- Implementing rewards and penalties
- Announcing your goals

A 90-Day Run will be critical to your success by providing the structure required to accomplish your goal. It will also help to eliminate the excuses so many people use, including the "I don't have enough time" excuse. In fact, your 90-Day Run will actually add back time by helping you to become more effective and efficient with your schedule.

The SCALE Factor will teach you how to invest about 3% of your day toward your weight-loss goal while maximizing your remaining 97%.

The first three weeks of your 90-Day Run will be the most challenging, but they are also the most crucial. This is when many people give up on their goals. I have found that when people follow a new pattern in their life for three consecutive weeks, it will become a new habit. And when people stop a pattern for three weeks, they can eliminate a habit.

The Marines understand this principle and divide boot camp into three phases to more effectively shape their young recruits. The first few weeks of Phase 1 are specifically designed to break civilian habits and prepare them for their new "Marine" habits. Civilian thoughts and behaviors are considered to be detrimental to training as a Marine, so they are eliminated during this period by intense physical activities, strict discipline, new routines, and demanding instructions.

My old patterns and habits ushered in the 216 pounds I saw on my scale. But my new patterns and habits led me directly to my weight-loss goal. I knew my ability to stay focused during my first three weeks would be most critical to accomplishing my goal. To lose weight, I would need the structure of a 90-Day Run to support my new patterns and habits.

In boot camp, I did not have access to unhealthy foods, so the temptation was not there. At home, it was a different story. I had junk food in the pantry and soda in the refrigerator. My family was not on a 90-Day Run, so those foods were present while I was striving to accomplish my goal. I also came across those foods at work, at the grocery store, and at restaurants.

Eliminating the presence of all unhealthy foods was impractical, so I did the next best thing. I sectioned off a portion of our pantry and designated a shelf in the refrigerator for my healthy foods. More than likely, you will not be able to pursue your weight-loss goal in an environment that is 100% set up to support you, like I experienced in boot camp. But you can set up parts of your environment that support your new patterns and habits.

REWARDS & PENALTIES

The right incentives will play a major role during your 90-Day Run. Both rewards and penalties will help to keep you focused and moving toward your goal. Let's say your goal is to lose 25 pounds. When you lose five pounds, do not reward yourself with a banana split; reward yourself with a new outfit. Choosing the appropriate rewards and penalties can provide the motivation necessary to accomplish your goal.

- Rewards — For taking steps toward your goal — developing new patterns
- Penalties — For taking steps away from your goal — eliminating old habits

During recruit training, we had many incentives. But for some reason, I seem to remember more of the penalties than the rewards. For recruits in boot camp, a motivating reward could be as simple as granting us additional time to write a letter to someone at home. It may not seem like a powerful reward, but when you are separated from your family, getting extra time to write a letter was a major incentive.

Penalties played a big part in our transformation. Even the smallest mistake may have caused our entire platoon to pay severely. We were often sent into a dirt pit to perform endless exercises, or we marched for additional hours. Being penalized took a heavy toll on our platoon, so we avoided it at all costs.

As a huge movie fan, I used rewards and penalties that pertained to watching movies, as some of my incentives to accomplish my goal. As I achieved small amounts of weight loss, I rewarded myself with a DVD. As a penalty, for not sticking to my diet and exercise routine, I donated a favorite movie to a charity.

Make sure that your incentives hold enough meaning to you. To work, they need to be motivating and inspirational. Rewards and penalties are valuable tools for your 90-Day Run. You can make these incentives fun and challenging.

Announcing Your Goals

If you want to put urgency on your efforts, shine the "spotlight" on you and your 90-Day Run. This is where you can enlist the help of others to support your goal. Make a list of people to whom you can announce your weight-loss goal. There is tremendous power in sharing your weight-loss goals with others. I shared my weight loss goals with family, friends, and certain co-workers.

The more people who know of your weight-loss goal, the more likely you are to accomplish it. To further ensure your success, let everyone on the list know the timelines of your 90-Day Run: start date, end date, midway milestone objectives, etc. People who know the details about your goals are more likely to ask questions about your progress. Intensely tracking your results will give you the ability to share great news when asked.

So, remember, when striving to lose weight, don't keep your goals a secret. A properly announced 90-Day Run will turn up the heat on your efforts and help to "melt" away those unwelcome pounds.

The SCALE Factor is designed to be the last program you use to accomplish your weight loss goal. Your 90-Day Run will provide you with all of the necessary support to stay the course and I am confident that you can accomplish your goal in 90 days.

Break out your calendar and list today as the "Day I Started My 90-Day Run." Fight the urge to start it later, even tomorrow. Remember, today is all you have. Identify the end of your first three weeks and list that day as "The Day I Completed My First 3 Weeks." Now, find day 90 and list it as "The Day I Completed My 90-Day Run, Accomplished My Goal, and Started a New Life."

If you would like some GREAT templates to help you complete your 90-Day Run, you can find them in my book, *The GOAL Formula* or check our GPS: Goal Planning Strategy - your full 90-Day Power Journal.

Visit our website: www.ThinkGreat90.com

Congratulations on controlling your thoughts and launching your 90-Day Run. Now, let's talk about some amazing food and the power you will experience when you **Control Your Menu**.

Factor 2 - Your Menu

"To eat is a necessity, but to eat healthy is an art."

— Francois dela Rochefoucauld

When I set my weight-loss goal, I was not a certified dietician, but I knew the "fuel" I was putting in my engine had a lot to do with the poor performance of my "vehicle." If I were to sum up my eating habits and the types of food I was consuming, I would have to say they were not great. In fact, they were not even good. Okay, without sugar-coating it, they were downright bad.

During my tour of duty with the Marine Corps, I was trained as an air traffic controller. Every day, I watched hundreds of unique military aircraft head out for training missions. Not all aircraft engines are designed the same, but they function similarly. Not all human bodies are designed the same, but they too, function similarly. Putting the right fuel in your engine is necessary to complete your mission: losing weight.

Regardless of their design, jet engines, sometimes referred to as gas turbines, all function on the same basic principle. The engine pulls air in at the front with a fan, while the compressor raises the pressure of the air. The blades compress the air, which is then sprayed with fuel. An electric spark ignites the mixture, causing the burning gases to expand. Pushed through the back of the engine, this process causes the aircraft to move forward.

Although there were dozens of different types of planes and helicopters, each one required the proper fuel to complete its mission. Like those aircraft, your body requires the right type of fuel to get moving, stay on course, and land successfully (on your scale). Understanding how your body functions and choosing the right foods, will help you to take off the weight and keep it off.

AVOID TURBULENCE

Since losing weight was an important goal for me, I wanted to identify anything that could slow me down. Just as pilots are aware of the impact of turbulence on their flights, you must be aware of the role your metabolism will play in your weight loss efforts. More importantly, you must get your metabolism to work toward your weight-loss goal, not against it.

Metabolism is the combination of chemical reactions which occur within any living cell or organism. It is a constant process that occurs from the time you are conceived until the time you die. The substances you provide to your body are broken down and converted to energy. This energy is used for vital processes; everything from thinking to eating to exercising, which are the three parts of **The SCALE Factor.**

Thousands of metabolic functions happen simultaneously, and every reaction is regulated by the body with a common outcome, in order to keep our cells healthy and functioning properly. It is estimated that the human body has approximately 100 trillion cells. That's a lot of cells to maintain. What are you feeding your cells?

For me, my extra weight was not the only thing that disappointed me. Although I had an amazing marriage, I was not happy with my life's overall direction. I felt as though I was at a standstill. Actually, the only thing that seemed to be moving was the dial on my scale. Unfortunately, it was moving in the wrong direction. It would be my focus on what I was eating that would start moving the dial on my scale in the direction I desired.

Like many people, I tried various diets in an attempt to lose weight. Although they helped me shed a few initial pounds, I soon discovered most diets cut out more than just bad foods. I found myself eliminating many foods which provided essential nutrients my body needed to thrive.

Gimmick-diets, such as low-carb, no-carb, high protein, and veggies-only may work for a short period. But most people on these programs eventually put back on all of the weight. An important part of my weight-loss goal included keeping the weight off. I wanted my goal to be life-changing, not just a temporary fix.

I discovered that eating a balanced diet consisting of proper carbohydrates, proteins, and essential fats, allowed me to eat well and lose weight at the same time. In fact, the first twenty pounds I lost was a direct result of eating better, not exercising. My scale shifted from 216 to 196 in one month, without picking up a single dumbbell or stepping onto a treadmill. I started to control the direction my scale was going as I started to control my menu.

THE BASIC MATH OF WEIGHT LOSS

By developing a better understanding of how my body was breaking down foods, I gained an edge in planning my meals and increasing my weight loss. Both weight gain and weight loss occur as a result of some basic math: your body must use up more calories than it consumes. Well, that was simple. But if it is so simple, why do people fail, even when they are on a diet? Let's take a closer look at the numbers.

A calorie can be defined as a unit of energy. Your body needs energy to perform basic and complex functions. Your objective is to provide your body with the correct number of calories to function properly. Any extra calories are stored as fat for future use. Weight gain occurs when we continue to consume more calories than our bodies can effectively process.

- 1 gram of protein contains 4 calories.
- 1 gram of carbohydrates contains 4 calories.
- 1 gram of fat contains 9 calories.
- 1 pound equals 3,500 calories.

To put that in perspective, let's look at the calorie count of a common meal from McDonald's[1].

Big Mac:	540 calories
Small French Fries:	230 calories
Medium Coca-Cola[2]:	210 calories
Total (one meal):	980 calories

To lose just one pound per week (3,500 calories), you need to reduce your caloric intake by 500 calories per day (for seven days). Many factors contribute to the eating problem each of us face on a daily basis. Not only will I explain the true problem, but I will show you why so many programs fail to work.

But the exciting part is that you will learn about the healthy foods which will help you to lose weight. You will be provided with great recipes for your 90-Day Run and your new lifestyle. You will understand how to schedule your daily meals to keep your metabolism working toward your new body.

---

[1] McDonald's and Big Mac are registered trademarks of McDonald's Corporation. Nutritional data from http://www.mcdonalds.com.
[2] Coca-Cola is a registered trademark of the Coca-Cola Company.

A "Growing" Problem

"A problem well stated is a problem half solved."

— Charles F. Kettering

I t has been well documented: our society has an eating problem. By definition, a "problem" is a question proposed for solution. To lose weight and keep it off, you must fully understand the reasons why people gain so much weight these days. We have become so accustomed to living with the problem that we manage to incorporate it into every aspect of our lives. But what is the problem?

You know the old saying, "What goes up, must come down." Too bad our weight does not work that easily. Sadly, many people eat as if it does. The reality is that what goes up, stays up, especially because of a "growing" eating problem I call **Processed Convenience**. Bad habits are hard to break but can be much more challenging when they appear to make our lives easier and more cost-effective (in the short-term).

Part of the problem is that some people are not aware of how unhealthy their eating habits actually are. Unhealthy eating is like driving your car with the check engine light on. If you do not identify the problem quickly, your drive may take longer than expected, be an unpleasant experience, or you could come to an abrupt halt.

It is estimated that nearly two-thirds of adults in America are overweight. In fact, according to the National Health and Nutrition Examination Surveys (NHANES), approximately 69% of adults are overweight or obese, with more than 78 million adult Americans considered obese. Most alarming is the rising number of obese children. According to the Centers for Disease Control, childhood obesity has more than doubled in children and quadrupled in adolescents in the past 30 years.

There is no doubt that people are trying to use various solutions to accomplish their weight loss goals, but their scales are continuing to point in the wrong direction. According to the Calorie Control Council, approximately 71 million people in the U.S. are currently on a diet. Interestingly enough, MedicineNet.com states that Americans spend an estimated $42 billion annually on weight loss foods, products, and services - with little results.

The eating epidemic in America does far more damage than just causing people to gain weight. It contributes to many health risks, such as:

- Heart disease
- Some forms of cancer
- Diabetes
- Stroke
- High blood pressure
- Sleep apnea and other breathing disorders
- Complications of pregnancy
- Psychological disorders, such as depression

Even one of these risks should cause someone to think twice about eating poorly, but people continue to be a part of this "growing" trend, and it could kill them, literally.

To keep up with our fast-paced lives, we have replaced an active lifestyle with being busy. We have replaced exercise with working more hours. And we have replaced healthy eating with processed convenience.

Three main factors work together to make the problem of processed convenience a deadly issue in our country:

- Quick and easy foods
- Misleading information
- Unscheduled meals

QUICK AND EASY FOODS

People are so busy these days that their diets tend to be based on convenience rather than health, and convenience is rarely healthy. Fast food restaurants not only make it easy to pick up a quick meal for lunch, but they make it inexpensive too. You can usually find some sort of combo meal for about $5. A cheeseburger, fries, and soda is the common choice. But you already know the math: $5 = 1,000 calories.

The art of making a grocery list is all but gone, replaced by the ease of buying ready-made frozen meals. In the last few years, there has been an explosion in the number of people "nuking" their food. Many people overlook the importance of preparing fresh, nutritious meals that taste great.

We have become conditioned to appreciate the taste of processed food over natural, fresh foods. Unfortunately, food manufacturers have included preservatives and additives into these foods to improve taste, keep water and fats from separating, and to prolong their shelf life. Okay, let's stop for a minute. Prolong shelf life? How can anything designed, and I do mean designed, to increase its shelf life, be good for you? If there is something in the food that prevents it from breaking down, wouldn't your body have a tough time breaking it down as well?

Food preservatives may contain or release formaldehyde which, among other things is carcinogenic (cancer-causing). When my schedule was at its most chaotic point, I became an expert in preparing a quick processed meal or picking up food from the drive-thru. Convenience eventually caught up to me and my scale. The time and money I thought I was saving, really was not worth it. It may cost you on all of the energy you lose, or worse yet, it may cost you on all of the medical bills you incur.

MISLEADING INFORMATION

Over the past 40 years, America has become more health conscious. Simultaneously, we have become fatter. How did that happen? Even with the most up-to-date medical information regarding healthy eating, people continue to eat the wrong foods. Perhaps that is because the wrong foods are packaged so wonderfully.

Just walk down the aisles at your local grocery store and read the "front of package" (FOP) labels. They can be confusing and entice the consumer to buy products which seem healthier than they actually are. Fat-free, low-fat, no additives, all natural, and sugar-free are just a few of the slogans used. Most people never discover what is really in their food.

One of the biggest causes of weight gain is the misconception that fat-free means calorie-free. It absolutely does not. Low-fat cookies may only have about 30% fewer calories than regular cookies. Studies have shown that people who eat fat-free or low-fat foods, generally eat larger portions. Always read the back label for the accurate nutritional information about your food.

Portion control is essential for losing weight, so check the serving size. Many people overlook this crucial information and eat 3-4 times as many calories than they thought. Can you guess how many calories are in a bag of chips? Let's take a look at one serving of Tostitos 100% White Corn Tortilla Chips with a Hint of Lime. Sounds very tasty, but...

Total calories for one serving: 150
Amount of chips per serving: 6

When was the last time you ate six chips and stopped? That is 25 calories per chip. Oh, by the way, the front of the bag also says "0 Grams Trans Fat." Wow, lucky you! FOP labels are designed with one purpose in mind: to convince you to buy their product by making you feel it is better for you than it actually is.

Tip of the SCALE — Eat slowly to give your body time to know when it has had enough. The human stomach takes about 20 minutes to register that it is "full."

UNSCHEDULED MEALS

One of the best ways to keep your metabolism going is to schedule your meals properly throughout the day. Your body is not designed to eat two or three large meals per day, but that is what most of us do. Your metabolism works best when the amount of food you eat is properly distributed throughout the day, starting with breakfast.

The first meal of the day is very important to get your body moving and your metabolism working. Think of breakfast as the meal that "breaks" the "fast" that your body has been going through while it was at rest during the night. As crucial as this meal is, it is estimated that over half of Americans do not eat breakfast.

Some people even skip lunch or eat something on the run. That was me. Then at night, I would load up on a big, tasty meal, just before bedtime. Rarely were my meals at the same time each day.

The idea that eating late in the evening will cause you to gain weight is controversial. If you eat a 500-calorie meal at 5:00 pm or eat the same meal at 10:00 pm, it has the same number of calories, right?

Yes, it does. But the real problem with eating in the evening is not the calories you eat, it is the calories you take to bed.

Going to sleep after eating a meal can have a significant impact on gaining weight. Let's take a look at an elite athlete who has mastered the art of scheduling his meals to accomplish his fitness goals. Sumo wrestlers weigh about 200 pounds when they start but can quickly weigh in between 300 and 400 pounds when they get to the top division.

One sumo wrestler from Hawaii, Konishiki Yasokichi, became a grand champion and tipped the scales at 600 pounds. These athletes have mastered the factors for quickly gaining weight. Simply, the sumo wrestler eats two enormous meals per day; then he sleeps. Sound familiar? I felt like I was becoming a sumo. I just didn't want to wear the outfit.

I was eating late in the evening, but I found my biggest problem was that I was going to sleep right after my meal. Snoozing after a meal can disrupt sleep in a number of ways. Many people suffer from gastroesophageal reflux, which causes a burning pain in the chest and throat. The late-night meal can also put pressure on the diaphragm, resulting in more snoring, which can often lead to a lack of air, thus less oxygen to the body and to the brain.

Tip of the SCALE
Schedule your meals to allow enough time (at least three hours) to pass before going to sleep.

Quick and easy foods, misleading information, and unscheduled meals will cause weight gain, increase health risks, and can potentially shorten life spans. Understanding what causes the "growing" problem of **Processed Convenience** forced me to take a closer look at what I was putting into my body.

Your body can only work with the food you supply it. Once I accepted that fact, I began to control my menu and my menu stopped controlling me. I switched from processed convenience to natural convenience.

Tip of the SCALE

If it is not included in Mother Nature's wrapper — stay away. Learning to prepare natural foods will prove to be more convenient and will help you to feel better.

The SCALE Factor can help you to lose weight, reduce the possibilities of health risks, and live a longer, healthier life.

FOOD FOR THOUGHT: THERE IS NO QUICK FIX

"If it looks too good to be true, it probably is."
— Conventional Wisdom

Today, everyone expects things fast, fast, fast. We have become a society of impatient people. Our computers can never start up quick enough, it always takes too long for the traffic light to turn green, and we end up standing in line for more than three minutes, for a $5 cup of coffee. We expect lightning-fast results with everything. I have even seen people lose their cool because their fast food was not prepared fast enough.

Unfortunately, most people expect the same quick results when it comes to losing weight. Part of this unrealistic expectation stems from infomercials, television commercials, and print ads promising viewers quick weight loss with little or no effort. Magazine covers are flooded with pictures of celebrities who dropped a lot of weight in a short period of time and headings that read "...and how you can too."

Fast food restaurants have jumped on the "fitness" bandwagon and some now offer "healthy" menus featuring reduced calorie items. Even though the foods on the healthy menus are better for you, I have seen too many people cave in when they get in the drive thru. It is not the healthy foods you can smell while waiting in line. It is the fried foods: burgers, fries, onion rings.

CHAPTER 6

Grocery stores now offer numerous diet and weight-loss items. In fact, they often have their own aisle, featuring low-calorie meals, vitamins, healthy shakes, and nutrition bars. I find it ironic that these "weight-loss" aisles are located so close to the aisles packed with the unhealthy food we consumed in the first place.

On a positive note, grocery stores are also packed with natural foods needed to properly lose weight and keep it off. Fresh vegetables, fresh fruits, and high-protein meats are readily available. These foods do not come in wrappers designed to convince you they are good for you. You know they are. We do not need a wrapper to convince us that eating fresh vegetables is good for us.

A general rule of thumb is to try and shop on the outer perimeter of the grocery store, where most of the fresh foods are located. The processed foods are typically in the center aisles. Even though the solution to weight loss is directly under people's noses, it is still more tempting to initially seek that quick fix.

WHEN DID I GET LIKE THIS?

Gaining weight is a relatively slow process. A combination of less activity and an increased consumption of unhealthy foods work together to give you the body you never expected. You cannot expect a quick fix to a long-term problem.

As I gained weight, my first fix was to buy bigger pants. I gradually went from a size 32 waist to a size 36. Sure, the bigger pants felt better than squeezing into my smaller ones, but I did not feel better about myself. In fact, I was slowly creeping up on a larger size. While I was shopping for clothes one day, I actually found myself staring at some of the bigger sizes, like 40 and above.

Realizing, as I stepped into the dressing room, that I may be trying on size 40 pants the next time I was here, I knew I was ready for a change.

I needed a permanent solution to my weight-gain problem. Like most people, I wanted to quickly take it all off and look like my old self again. I looked for the "quick-fix" programs and easily found many. Although I discovered numerous options, I found few solutions for my weight-loss goal. I was determined to lose weight and keep it off.

QUICK FIXES = QUICK FAILURES

Almost everyone who has failed to accomplish their weight loss goal, did experience some initial success. Weight-loss programs typically help people to drop between 5-10 pounds rather quickly, causing a false sense of security that the program will work over the long-haul. Unfortunately, their initial weight loss is usually a result of losing water and depleted muscle mass, not fat.

Those pounds quickly return, and another program is attempted. The cycle continues and yet another program is sought. Hopping from one program to the next, they frustratingly lose and gain the same 5-10 pounds. Desperate to permanently lose weight, most people are willing to try just about anything, even quick fixes.

- Fad diets
- Weight-loss pills
- Weight-loss surgery

Despite warnings from medical professionals and nutrition experts, people still seek out all forms of quick fixes to shed excess weight: fad diets, weight-loss pills, and even risky surgery. These fixes may provide temporary weight loss, but not the permanent solutions you need to maintain proper weight or promote a healthy lifestyle.

These quick fixes may not only cause you to fail at your long-term weight-loss goal, but they may cause some long-term damage to your body.

We live in a society obsessed with celebrities and their perfect physiques. Television shows, radio programs, and the tabloids all feature stories about celebrities who quickly lost weight and talk about the "remarkable new diet plan they used." The before and after pictures from these trendy diets are too good to resist and many people jump right into them.

Kirstie Alley lost a tremendous amount of weight on the Jenny Craig program, only to put it back on. The headlines quickly switched from details of her weight loss to details of Jenny Craig dropping her as their spokesperson for fear that people will stop using their program.

Oprah Winfrey has admittedly struggled with weight gain and has had temporary success with different diets, including a high protein liquid diet that helped her to "temporarily" lose 67 pounds in 1988. According to Oprah, "I had literally starved myself for four months, not a morsel of food, to get into that pair of size 10 Calvin Klein jeans." "Two hours after that show, I started eating to celebrate, of course, within two days those jeans no longer fit," (USAToday.com, 2005).

Singer and actress, Beyoncé, dropped 20 pounds in 2 weeks on the Master Cleanse Diet, which consists of fasting, where you eat no solid foods and drink 6-12 glasses of water mixed with lemon juice, maple syrup and cayenne pepper for 10-40 days. As soon as she stopped the diet, she quickly gained all of the weight back and admitted to being unhappy while she was on the diet. Beyoncé said, "As soon as it was over, I gained the weight back; I ate everything when it was over... the second I looked at a donut, it came back. I gained back all the weight."

Many other fad diets lure people into thinking they can easily take off the weight. There are numerous versions of these unhealthy diets: liquid diets, the grapefruit diet, low-carb diet, and the protein diet.

They all have one thing in common; the weight you take off comes back. Then you are starting all over again, looking for the next fad diet.

Fast weight loss and weight gain is not healthy. Fad diets often lead to frustration and discouragement. They also deprive you of essential vitamins and nutrients a healthy body requires. Controlling your thoughts, eating a balanced diet, and exercising properly (Part III) will provide you with everything your body was designed for.

 Tip of the SCALE Avoid fad diets at all costs. Do not be trendy, be healthy.

WEIGHT-LOSS PILLS

Going back to the fast, fast, fast mentality, diet pills are a favorite choice of many people. Pop the "magic pill" and the weight will just melt away. It wasn't a pill that put the weight on, and it won't be a pill that takes it off.

According to National Business Journal, $1.7 billion was spent on weight-loss pills in 2007. A survey from the Centers for Disease Control (CDC) found that women were more than twice as likely as men to buy them. The bottom line is, these pills are unhealthy.

The Food and Drug Administration continues to crack down on weight-loss pills, believing a large percentage of them are tainted. Michael Levy, current FDA Acting Director of the agency's division of new drugs and labeling compliance says, "We have ramped up our investigation of these types of products as a result of initial samples." He added, "I think a large percentage of these products are tainted."

Despite the finding from the FDA and the negative press diet pills receive, it is still a popular quick fix. It has been estimated that 30% of teenage girls have used diet pills at some point. According to the American Dietetic Association, spending on weight-loss products in the U.S. continues to grow even though many of these products come with significant health risks, and no guarantee of results.

Because many diet pills use stimulants to boost your metabolism, one of the most dangerous effects is heart-related. Other diet pills promote weight loss by tricking your body into feeling full. While losing weight through diet pills can deprive your body of essential vitamins and nutrients, it is also known to raise your blood pressure, which increases the risk of heart attack and stroke.

Tip of the SCALE   Stay away from diet pills.

WEIGHT-LOSS SURGERY

Weight-loss surgery is an extreme quick fix and in many cases, irreversible. For some people, especially those who are morbidly obese, or those with health conditions, surgery may be the only option. Unfortunately, there is an increase in weight-loss surgeries for people who have stopped trying to accomplish their weight-loss goal by changing their patterns and habits.

Many people are turning to weight-loss surgery too quickly and the constant addition of new medical procedures does not help this quick-fix problem.

Weight-Loss surgery can have some very drastic risks and side effects:

- **Vomiting:** restrictive surgery causes the small stomach to be overly stretched by food particles that have not been well chewed.
- **"Dumping Syndrome":** stomach contents move too rapidly through the small intestine and can cause nausea, weakness, sweating, faintness and, occasionally, diarrhea after eating. Also, it creates the inability to eat sweets without becoming extremely weak.
- **Nutritional Deficiencies:** anemia, osteoporosis, and metabolic bone disease are common, but can be avoided if vitamin and mineral intakes are constantly maintained.
- **Complications:** follow-up operations may be required to correct complications such as abdominal hernias, infections, breakdown of the staple line (used to make the stomach smaller) and stretched stomach outlets (when the stomach returns to its normal size).
- **Gallstones:** More than one-third of obese patients who have gastric surgery develop gallstones.

Weight-loss surgery always requires drastic lifestyle changes after the procedure. Most patients require close monitoring and also need to follow a life-long diet and exercise program. The bad eating habits that added weight before surgery can create significant health issues after surgery.

In addition, women who have this surgery need to avoid pregnancy until their weight becomes stable. Rapid weight loss and nutritional deficiencies are detrimental to a developing fetus.

Weight-loss surgery is costly, but not as costly as failing to follow the new lifestyle changes required to survive. If someone did not have the ability to control their thoughts, their menu, and their body before the surgery, how can they be expected to permanently change it after the surgery?

There is nothing wrong with wanting to lose weight quickly. Just remember that you do not want to do more damage to your body in the process.

Tip of the SCALE Make the investment in changing your lifestyle to prevent ending up on the operating table.

The SCALE Factor will show you how to implement easy-to-follow lifestyle changes now. Many people do not eat healthy because they do not understand that simple meals can have great results. I will show you how to prepare healthy meals and do it faster and more cost-effective than a fast food restaurant. In today's economy, imagine saving more money than you would by ordering fast food, and it's healthy.

The SCALE Factor will teach you how to get back on the natural program your body was designed for.

YOU ARE WHAT YOU EAT

"The first wealth is health."

— Ralph Waldo Emerson

Our bodies may seem complex, but they are very simple. The human body is great at doing exactly what we tell it to do. When we eat unhealthy foods and fail to exercise, our bodies respond accordingly. But when we nourish them with healthy foods and maintain consistent activity, we acquire healthier bodies and a greater life.

To understand how to make the body work, you must first understand how the body functions. Here is the highly complex, medical definition: our bodies are just a bunch of cells. That being said, it is in our best interest to provide those cells exactly what they need in order to do their jobs effectively and efficiently. When we make their job harder than it needs to be, we will always pay the price.

Our bodies are comprised of approximately 100 trillion cells, which are broken down into 150 different groups: blood cells, skin cells, heart cells, etc. Although they all perform different functions, they do have something in common. Cells do not last forever. They constantly die and replace themselves over our entire life span. It is happening right now, to millions of your cells, as you read this book.

Red blood cells die and replace themselves every 90 days, while skin cells do the same thing every 21-28 days. Our heart cells are completely replaced every eight months, while the cells of our bones can take up to ten years.

In essence, we have a new body every 7-10 years. But new does not always translate into healthier for many people. Your body does its job. You need to do yours.

In order to perform the function of regeneration, your body is relying on you to supply it with all of the proper materials: food, nutrients, and water. Most people just do not understand what their bodies require. With the right knowledge, they are usually more than willing to stop feeding their bodies (and their family's bodies) harmful foods, and start supplying them with healthy choices.

By providing your body with a menu of life-changing foods, you will not only allow it to rebuild itself, you will become healthier and you will accomplish your weight-loss goal quicker. Your new menu must consist of: carbohydrates, proteins, fats, vitamins & minerals, and fiber. And don't forget to wash it all down with a lot of water. We will discuss the benefits of water in the next section.

A healthy body requires these elements, just as your car requires gas, oil, transmission fluid, and brake fluid to run properly. Try driving your car without oil and see how far you get.

Thousands of books have been written regarding how the various elements of your diet benefit your body. For now, I will provide you with a basic overview. Then, we will discuss which foods provide you with these valuable resources and how to make healthy meals that taste great and help you to lose weight.

WATER

Water is the most important resource in your body and must be included consistently in your menu. You can survive for weeks without food but you can last only 5-7 days without water. In boot camp, we carried two full canteens of water with us, each holding 32 ounces. We went through both canteens each day, and then some.

Aside from a little milk and juice at the chow hall, we only consumed water.

The human body is roughly 60% water in adult males and 55% water in adult females. Your bones are comprised of 22% water, blood contains 50% water, and your brain is about 75% water.

Even the slightest decrease in your body's water level will cause you to feel it.

Reduced by 1%:	Thirsty
Reduced by 5%:	Hot and tired
Reduced by 10%:	Delirium (temporary mental confusion) and blurred vision
Reduced by 20%:	Death

Far too many people do not drink pure water on a daily basis. They have replaced water with alternatives such as coffee, tea, and soda. Flavored waters and energy drinks have also started to replace natural water. In fact, the sizes of soft drinks continue to grow, and people are hydrating themselves with large amounts of unhealthy beverages. Big Gulp was introduced by 7-11 convenience stores in 1980 and has since grown to 64 ounces, which is half a gallon of soda, that might total over 700 calories.

Those drinks do not supply your body with the water it needs, and they add on a lot of weight. Studies have also shown that people who drink soda have a lower bone mineral density because most colas contain phosphoric acid and caffeine, which depletes calcium from the bones. In addition to numerous other risks, they are high in sugars, particularly high fructose corn syrup (HFCS), which causes dehydration. Drinking a soda to quench your thirst will actually make you thirstier.

Every day, we lose 2-3 quarts of water. It is up to us to replenish our bodies with water throughout the day. So, how much water should we drink? Water intake varies based on many factors. A person's size and level of activity are important to keep in mind. Some experts suggest drinking eight, 8-ounce glasses of water per day. The latest formula suggests that we drink half our body weight in ounces of water each day. A person who weighs 120 pounds should drink 60 ounces of water, while a person who weighs 200 pounds should drink 100 ounces of water each day.

A general guide to making sure you drink the right amount of water is the color of your urine, which should be pale yellow. Not the most exciting way to track your water intake, but your body knows what it needs.

Tip of the
SCALE
Drink half of your glass of water before eating your meal — it will help to control your appetite.

CARBOHYDRATES

Main Function: To provide our bodies with energy.

Carbohydrates play a vital role in the proper functioning of our brain, heart, nervous system, digestive system and immune system. Carbs are essential for our bodies in many ways, but numerous fad diets have presented them as one of the enemies of weight loss.

Carbohydrates are a combination of oxygen, hydrogen and carbon. They are especially used to provide energy to the brain and to the central nervous system. Some diets suggest that we eliminate them entirely. Remember, most weight-loss plans help you to shed 5-10 pounds, which is the same weight that returns quickly.

Increasing the right amount of carbohydrates in our diet can actually contribute to weight loss. A banana has roughly 100 calories, as does a can of soda. Eating the banana will not only give you energy but will help to satisfy your hunger. A soda has no nutritional benefits, but the average American drinks 57 gallons per year.

Carbohydrates can be categorized into two groups:

Simple Carbohydrates: Quickly absorbed by the body and are found in foods such as refined sugars, milk and some fruits. Stay away from simple carbohydrate foods such as soda, cake, chocolate, and candy. Some simple carbohydrates are found in certain types of fresh fruits and vegetables, which will provide you with valuable nutrients. For example, milk is a simple carbohydrate that provides calcium.

Complex Carbohydrates: Fiber-rich, they are digested more slowly. There is no limit to the amount of nutritional benefits you get from switching to complex carbohydrates. These foods contain vitamins, minerals, and other nutrients that are rarely present in simple-sugar food items. Good sources of carbohydrates include potatoes, fruits, rice, yams, spaghetti, breads, and cereals. You must balance the amount of carbohydrates you eat. Too little will cause you to feel tired; too much and your body stores them as fat.

Foods high in complex carbohydrates are often lower in calories. They make great snacks throughout the day. Your menu needs to include carbohydrates in order for you to properly lose weight.

Fiber is an important form of carbohydrate that comes only from plant-based foods such as fruits, vegetables and grains. It assists with the digestive process and is an essential element for the elimination of waste and toxins from our bodies. Fiber helps to keeps our intestines clean and disease-free. Dietary fiber is found in plant-based foods such as cereals, fruits and vegetables. Comprised of the indigestible parts of the plant, fiber has also been referred to as "roughage."

Published every five years since 1980, The 2010 Dietary Guidelines for Americans recommend that 45-65 percent of total daily calories be from carbohydrates.

According to the American Dietetic Association (ADA), adults need between 20 and 35 grams of fiber every day. Unfortunately, the organization reports that Americans currently eat between 12 and 17 grams per day.

There are two types of fibers: soluble and non-soluble.

1. **Soluble Fiber:** Controls blood sugar and may also lower cholesterol
2. **Non-Soluble Fiber:** Maintains bowel functions and may help reduce the risk of colon cancer

GOOD SOURCES OF SOLUBLE FIBER:

- Oat bran and oatmeal
- Beans and legumes
- Peas and carrots
- Soy
- Avocado
- Brown rice
- Barley
- Strawberries
- Bananas

GOOD SOURCES OF NON-SOLUBLE FIBER:

- Whole-wheat breads, cereals, and bran
- Granola
- Barley
- Melons
- Cabbage
- Brussels sprouts
- Nuts
- Cauliflower
- Fruits and vegetables with skin

PROTEINS

Function: To assist our bodies with growth and repair.

Protein is a vital part of our bodies, yet most people do not understand how necessary it is to incorporate it into their diet. If we do not eat enough protein, our bodies cannot grow properly and will be unable to heal from wounds and injuries. Exercising with weight training causes our muscles to tear (in a good way), then rebuild themselves stronger. Protein is required for this.

Because proteins are large molecules, they cannot go directly into our blood. Our digestive system turns them into amino-acids first. Once they are in our system, our bodies can convert the amino-acids into glucose (blood sugar), which can also provide us with energy.

Specialized proteins in our cells are the building blocks of our muscles. Providing our muscles with the right food is critical when doing day-to-day activities. Our cardiac muscles, also known as our hearts, constantly pump blood throughout our bodies and to our brains. What are you feeding your heart?

Specialized bodily functions occur because of proteins that interact in our blood: digestion, blood clotting, breathing, and our immune system all rely on our intake of foods rich in protein. Even our DNA uses proteins to reproduce and synthesize more DNA.

The enzymes in our stomachs break down proteins during digestion to provide essential amino acids.

FOODS HIGH IN PROTEIN:

- Meat
- Fish
- Egg whites
- Milk
- Peas
- Black beans
- Tofu
- Oats
- Nuts
- Soybeans

Function: To provide us with energy and fat-soluble vitamins.

Americans are conditioned to fear fats. Fats have been linked to cancer, heart disease, and other health risks. Of course, food manufacturers have responded with a "fat-free" version of everything from chips to cookies. Remember, fat-free does not mean calorie-free.

Avoiding fat in your diet will not keep you in shape. Fats can raise and lower your cholesterol levels. A balanced diet is about eating the essential fats your body needs.

There are "bad" fats and "good" fats. As you may have guessed, you need to avoid the bad fats and begin to incorporate the good fats into your menu. Because most people who want to lose weight do not understand the difference between bad and good fats, they avoid them both. Good fats are essential for your body and assist with the accomplishment of your goal.

Foods high in BAD Fats: marbled meats, sausage, bacon, French fries, microwave popcorn, vegetable shortening.

Foods high in GOOD Fats: nuts, fish, olives, avocados.

Bad fats, such as saturated fats can raise cholesterol levels and increase the risk of heart disease. Cholesterol is extremely important for good health and it helps the body to function properly by holding cells together. It also makes vitamin D, hormones, and substances that help our digestive system. Once again, we have been conditioned to fear cholesterol.

Our bodies actually make most of the cholesterol they need (about 75%) in the liver. The rest (about 25%) comes from animal products, such as chicken, beef, fish, and whole milk. While our bodies need this substance to work properly, too much of it can cause health problems.

There are two types of cholesterol: Bad and Good. Simple, huh?

1. Bad – Low-Density Lipoprotein (LDL)

LDL (bad) cholesterol circulates in the blood and can slowly build up in the inner walls of the arteries, restricting blood flow to the heart and brain. Arteries can become narrow and less flexible. A heart attack or stroke can result if a clot forms and blocks a narrowed artery. Your menu needs to eliminate BAD cholesterol.

2. Good – High-Density Lipoprotein (HDL)

HDL cholesterol is known as "good" cholesterol because high levels of HDL protect against heart attack. Your menu needs to maintain and balance GOOD cholesterol.

VITAMINS AND MINERALS

Function: to keep you healthy and are necessary for your teeth, bones, and muscles.

TYPES OF VITAMINS:

- Vitamin A   good for your eyes
- Vitamin B   helps to break down carbohydrates and provides energy
- Vitamin C   helps fight colds and aids in the healing process
- Vitamin D   contributes to bone and joint health
- Vitamin E   helps the circulatory system and fights cell damage

TYPES OF MINERALS:

- Iron   carries oxygen throughout the bloodstream
- Calcium   contributes to bone health and heart health
- Sodium   helps to hold water in body tissues
- Iodine   helps produce hormones for growth and development

Vitamins and minerals are needed in minor amounts, but they play a major role in allowing our bodies to function properly.

Free Radicals — Free radicals are the main cause of our bodies' aging process. A free radical is an unstable molecule, which steals electrons from other molecules. This process can start a chain reaction which leads to the damage of many important molecules in our cells. Free radicals are produced naturally by our bodies during normal metabolism and by factors in our environment. Unhealthy diets, smoking, pollutants, and ultra-violet rays from the sun all produce free radicals. "Oxidative" free radicals can be neutralized with the help of antioxidants.

Antioxidants — Antioxidants help protect our bodies from the damage of free radicals by slowing or preventing the oxidation of molecules. People who have diets with high levels of antioxidants have a lower risk of heart disease and neurological diseases. The Oxygen Radical Absorbance Capacity (ORAC) is a method used to measure the antioxidant capacities in foods. Foods proven to be high in antioxidants include fruits, vegetables, beans, cereals, nuts, and certain spices such as cinnamon.

Now you should have a better understanding of the key elements you need to feed your body. When our menu options provide our bodies the right foods, they will do everything they were designed to do, including getting back into shape. Now let's take a look at some quick, easy, and healthy meals that you can incorporate into your new menu.

THE RECIPES FOR LOSING WEIGHT

"You will never get out of the pot or pan anything fundamentally better than what went into it."

— Martha McCulloch-Williams

I love to eat, plain and simple. So, I needed to prepare appetizing and healthy meals that I would not get tired of eating. People quickly stop their weight-loss programs because diet foods can range from almost tasteless to downright horrible. You cannot stay on a meal plan you do not like.

In order to accomplish my weight-loss goal, I sought out foods that were healthy, tasty and worked together to shed my unwanted pounds.

Processed foods provide our bodies with empty calories and minimal nutrients, but they are designed to provide maximum taste. More than merely skimping on nutrients, bad foods also add many harmful elements to our bodies. When you take your car for a ride, you must watch out for hazards such as potholes, roadblocks, detours, and other drivers. Taking our bodies for a ride is no different. Each day, there are hazards to our health that must be avoided as well.

A balanced diet will do much more than help your body to function properly and get back into shape. A GREAT menu will also supply you with plenty of antioxidants to help fight the effects of free radicals in your body.

Designing Your Menu

When you begin the exciting process of planning a healthy menu, you become more aware of the foods you are putting into your body and the benefits you will receive from them. As I help people with their goal of losing weight, I find that most of them rarely plan their meals, let alone think about what harmful materials they may be consuming. Quickly planning our meals in the drive-thru rarely provides us with an opportunity to examine the contents of these "convenient" meals.

Now that you have a better understanding of the helpful and harmful elements you can put into your body, let's take a look at an example of a basic drive-thru dinner and a quick snack. Let's grab a sandwich and dessert. We will drive to Quiznos for a tuna sandwich and Baskin Robbins for an ice cream shake.

Quiznos Large Tuna Melt – (without chips and a soda) $7

- 2,090 calories
- 175 g fat (31 grams saturated fat, 2.5 grams trans fats)

Baskin Robbins Large Chocolate Oreo Shake $5

- 2,600 calories
- 135 g fat (59 grams saturated fat, 2.5 grams trans fats)

For about $12, you just became the proud owner of 4,690 calories, and 310 grams of fat in ONE meal. Remember, this did not include a drink or chips. I have seen people eat more in one sitting than mentioned above.

The average person requires about 2,000 calories per day and this single meal is more than double those calories. Guess what happens to all of those excess calories? Now, imagine eating that right before going to sleep. Hello sumo wrestler! Your metabolism can never compete with that type of calorie onslaught. Was it really worth the perceived savings? Was it really convenient?

The SCALE Factor provides you with the tasty and healthy meals that are less expensive than fast food and more convenient. Spend less, get more nutritional value, and lose weight. What a bargain.

The biggest key to a successful meal is FRESH, FRESH, FRESH!

Tip of the SCALE

When shopping in a grocery store, stick to the outer perimeter of the store where mostly non-processed, non-prepackaged foods are found.

GREAT MEALS

There are literally thousands of theories, philosophies, and old-wives tales about what to eat, when to eat, and how to eat. There are unlimited numbers of books, articles, and online reports with all of the latest and greatest research findings.

The following recipes are examples of the meals I prepared to increase my intake of healthy foods, which helped me to accomplish my personal weight-loss goal. They fit into my busy schedule and were more cost-effective than any fast food.

I particularly like them because I can make larger quantities and put the extra portions aside for future meals. With most of these recipes, I could make 4-6 meals for the week, which was truly a time-saving benefit for me. Feel free to experiment with each recipe but avoid substituting healthy ingredients with unhealthy ones.

Each menu item will include:

- Prep time
- Servings
- Cost per serving
- Easy-to-follow instructions

Egg White Scramble

Prep time: 45 minutes

Servings: 8

Cost per serving: $3.16

Ingredients

1-pound turkey sausage

2 tablespoons olive oil

1 red bell pepper, chopped

1 green bell pepper, chopped

1/2-pound mushrooms, sliced

6 green onions, diced fine

2 Roma tomatoes, diced

1 tablespoon diced jalapeños

(if desired)

1 (32 ounce) carton egg whites

Directions

Heat pan on medium-high. Lightly spray with non-stick cooking spray and cook the turkey sausage for about 10 minutes, or until cooked all the way through. Cut into bite-size pieces and set aside in a bowl. Heat pan on medium. Add 1 tablespoon olive oil. Add bell peppers, mushrooms, and onions. Cook for 5 minutes. Add tomatoes and jalapeños and cook for another 3 minutes. Set aside in a bowl.
Heat pan on medium-high. Spray with a light coating of cooking spray. Pour in egg whites and stir consistently until they are almost set. Add in the sausage and the vegetables. Cook for another few minutes. Serve with fresh fruit. Enjoy your meal.

Tip of the SCALE

Try different combinations of lean meats and vegetables to create your own unique dish.

Chicken Veggie Soup

Prep time: 55 minutes

Servings: 12

Cost per serving: $1.92

Ingredients

1 ½ pounds chicken breast

1 tablespoon canola oil

1 large onion, chopped

2½ cups celery, chopped

2½ cups carrots, chopped

2½ cups zucchini squash, chopped

8 cups water

1 teaspoon salt

1 teaspoon ground oregano

1 teaspoon thyme

2 vegetable bouillon cubes

1 (15 ounce) can garbanzo beans

1 (15 ounce) can red beans

1 (14.5 ounce) can Italian green beans

2 (14.5 ounce) cans tomatoes, diced

Directions

In a separate pot, boil chicken breast until fully cooked, about 15 minutes. Cut into bite-size pieces.

In a large pot, heat 1 tablespoon canola oil, coating the bottom. Cook the onions for 5 minutes, stirring occasionally. Add the celery, carrots, and zucchini squash and cook for another 5 minutes.

Pour in 8 cups of water and turn the heat on high. Stir in salt, oregano, thyme, and bouillon cubes. Bring to a boil.

Drain the garbanzo beans, red beans, and Italian green beans. Stir in with the diced tomatoes (undrained). Simmer for 5 minutes. Add chicken and simmer 5 more minutes. Serve with fruit. Bon Appétit.

Tip of the SCALE

Experiment by adding your favorite veggies. You can also add a few boiled potatoes once the soup is finished cooking. Freeze extra leftovers for later.

Cajun Salmon and Asparagus

Prep time: 25 minutes

Servings: 4

Cost per serving: $4.54

Ingredients

1 lemon

4 salmon fillets

Cajun seasoning to taste

1-pound fresh asparagus

½ tablespoon olive oil

Directions

Sprinkle juice from the lemon onto salmon fillets. Lightly sprinkle with Cajun seasoning to taste.
Pre-heat oven to 375° F. Bake salmon in a shallow baking sheet, on parchment paper, for 15-20 minutes or until flaky. Adjust oven to 450° F.
Wash asparagus and trim the rough ends. Apply some olive oil to asparagus and use your hands to rub it on. Sprinkle lightly with salt to taste.
Bake for about 10 minutes. Serve with fresh fruit.
Enjoy.

Tip of the SCALE

If you do not like it spicy, substitute the Cajun seasoning with lemon-pepper, or just sprinkle the salmon with lemon juice.

Turkey Chili and Red Potatoes

Prep time: 60 minutes

Servings: 8

Cost per serving: $2.52

Ingredients

1-pound red potatoes, sliced

1 tablespoon olive oil

1 onion, chopped

3 cloves garlic, chopped

1 teaspoon salt

2 teaspoons chili powder

1 teaspoon ground oregano

1-pound ground turkey

2 (14.5 ounce) cans tomatoes, diced

2 tablespoons tomato paste

1 cup red wine (alcohol will burn off)

1 (15 ounce) can red beans

4 green onions, chopped fine
Low-fat Monterey Jack cheese

1 avocado

Directions

Pre-heat oven to 350° F. Wash and slice red potatoes, about ½ inch thick. Place in a baking dish and bake for 30 minutes or until tender.

Heat olive oil in a large skillet over medium-high heat. Add onion, garlic, salt, chili powder, and oregano. Cook for 3 minutes. Add in ground turkey and cook until brown.

Stir in diced tomatoes, tomato paste, and red wine. Add beans and onions. Reduce heat and simmer for 15 minutes.

Sprinkle lightly with shredded Monterey Jack cheese and add sliced avocado. Serve red potatoes on the side.

Serve with fresh fruit. Enjoy.

Tip of the SCALE

Add more or less chili powder based on how hot you like it. Or add additional items such as jalapeños and Ortega chilis.

Grilled Chicken Caesar Salad Wrap

Prep time: 25 minutes

Servings: 4

Cost per serving: $2.62

Ingredients

1-pound thin, boneless, skinless chicken breasts

Low-fat Caesar salad dressing

4 wheat tortillas, small

4 lettuce leaves, or more

1 large tomato, sliced

1 medium onion, sliced

½ cup croutons - crushed

Directions

Heat grill over a medium-high flame. Grill chicken until cooked throughout, about 15 minutes depending on the thickness of the chicken breasts.
Lightly spread salad dressing on wheat tortilla.
Add strips of chicken breast, lettuce, tomato slices, and onion slices. Sprinkle with crushed croutons and fold tortilla.
Serve with fresh fruit.
Bon Appétit.

Tip of the SCALE

Make your own unique "chicken salad" wrap by selecting other ingredients that appeal to your taste.

Grilled Lemon Chicken and Squash

Prep time: 25 minutes

Servings: 4

Cost per serving: $2.93

Ingredients

1-pound, thin boneless, skinless chicken breasts

1 lemon

Salt and pepper to taste

2 medium yellow squash, sliced

¼ cup canola oil

Seasoning to taste

Directions

Heat grill over a medium-high flame. Grill chicken until cooked all the way through, about 15 minutes depending on the thickness of the chicken breasts.

Sprinkle chicken with lemon juice and add salt and pepper to taste.

Cut squash in half, horizontally. You don't want them to fall through the grill.

Lightly coat the squash with canola oil and sprinkle with desired seasoning.

Grill squash for about 7 minutes per side, or until desired tenderness.

Serve with fresh fruit. Enjoy.

Tip of the SCALE

Try sprinkling lime juice instead of lemon. Substitute other seasonings in lieu of salt and pepper.

Turkey Patty and Baked Veggies

Prep time: 45 minutes

Servings: 4

Cost per serving: $4.01

Ingredients

4 turkey patties

2 cups potatoes, peeled and cubed

2 cups carrots, 1-inch slices

2 cups fresh broccoli

2 cups zucchini, sliced

1 tablespoon olive oil

Season to taste

Directions

Pre-heat oven to 400° F.
Combine vegetables in a baking dish and add olive oil. Add desired seasoning to taste and mix.
Bake veggies for 30 minutes, or until tender.
Spray pan with cooking spray and place over medium-high heat. Add turkey patties and cook about 5 minutes on each side. Add salt and pepper to taste.
Serve with fruit. Enjoy your meal.

Tip of the SCALE

To add flavor to your turkey, substitute the salt and pepper with other seasonings or add a few drops of hot sauce.

Quick and Easy Crab Salad

Prep time: 10 minutes

Servings: 4

Cost per serving: $3.19

Ingredients

1 head of dark leaf lettuce, chopped

1 large tomato, diced

1 red onion, chopped

Vinaigrette dressing

1-pound imitation crab

1 avocado

Directions

Mix lettuce, tomato, and onion in a bowl. Add a small amount of vinaigrette dressing to taste and mix.
Add imitation crab, in bite-size pieces. Top with the sliced avocado.
Serve with fresh fruit. "Bon Appétit"

Tip of the SCALE Substitute crab meat with pre-cooked chicken or turkey.

Apple Chicken Salad

Prep time: 30 minutes

Servings: 4

Cost per serving: $4.21

Ingredients

1-pound, thin, boneless, skinless chicken breasts

1 pound fresh spinach

¼ cup red onion, chopped

2 apples (your choice), chopped

2 cups dried cranberries

¾ cup pecans

¼ cup low-fat Gorgonzola cheese

1 avocado

Directions

Pre-heat oven to 350° F.
Bake chicken for 25 minutes, or until cooked throughout.
Cut the chicken into bite-size pieces.
In a large bowl, combine spinach, onions, apples, cranberries, and pecans. Mix in chicken.
Top with Gorgonzola cheese and avocado slices.
Your fruit is in the salad already. Enjoy.

Tip of the SCALE

Substitute the spinach with other types of dark-leaf lettuce.

Teriyaki Chicken and Green Beans

Prep time: 25 minutes

Servings: 4

Cost per serving: $3.37

Ingredients

1-pound, thin, boneless, skinless chicken breasts

Low-fat Teriyaki sauce

1 pound of fresh green beans

1 tablespoon olive oil

1 fresh pineapple sliced

Salt and pepper to taste

Directions

Heat grill over a medium-high flame. Lightly coat the chicken with a low-fat Teriyaki sauce. Grill chicken until cooked all the way through, about 15 minutes depending on the thickness of the chicken breasts.

Wash green beans. Apply small amount of olive oil to lightly coat green beans. Sprinkle sparingly with salt to taste.

Using a BBQ grill skillet, grill green beans for about 10 minutes, or until tender.

Lightly coat pineapple slices with Teriyaki sauce and grill each side for a few minutes.

Enjoy your meal.

Tip of the SCALE

This meal can also be prepared in the oven in about 25 minutes by baking the chicken at 375° F.

Italian Crab Bake

Prep time: 60 minutes

Servings: 4

Cost per serving: $3.12

Ingredients

8 lasagna noodles, whole grain

2 egg whites

1-pound imitation crab

¼ cup low-fat Parmesan cheese, shredded

1 jar of spaghetti sauce

Directions

Boil lasagna noodles until tender. Rinse noodles in cool water; then lay them flat.
Separate the egg whites from 2 eggs.
Mix crab meat, cheese, and egg whites in a bowl.
On each noodle, add ½ cup of your mixed ingredients. Roll the noodles and place in a lightly greased baking dish.
Pour spaghetti sauce over noodles and sprinkle with a small amount of Parmesan cheese.
Bake at 375°F for 45 minutes.
Allow dish to sit for about 15 minutes.
Serve with salad and fresh fruit.

Tip of the SCALE

You can substitute stewed tomatoes for the spaghetti sauce and chicken for the crab meat. Adding a little spaghetti sauce to the bottom of the baking dish helps to prevent the lasagna from sticking to the dish.

Cinnamon Apple Crisp

Prep time: 40 minutes

Servings: 4

Cost per serving: $0.50

Ingredients

¼ cup apple juice or apple cider

2 cups applesauce

Dash ground cinnamon

2 small to medium apples

1 tablespoon brown sugar

½ cup granola

Directions

In a mixing bowl, combine apple juice, apple sauce, brown sugar, and cinnamon.
Slice apples and place in mixing bowl with the combined ingredients, covering apple slices with the mixture.
Pour mixture and apples into a baking dish.
Bake, covered, at 350°F for 30 minutes or until apples are tender.
Let cool for 5 minutes. Sprinkle granola on top.
Enjoy your healthy dessert.

Tip of the SCALE

Try switching out the apples for peaches for a unique taste.

Quick and Easy

Cottage Cheese & Fruit

Servings – 1

Time to make – 1-minute

Cost per serving – $1.45

½ cup of cottage cheese and a handful of fruit make a perfect quick breakfast. Add a glass of water for a great meal.

Healthy Sandwich

Servings – 1

Time to make – 5 minutes

Cost per serving – $1.35

Add a few slices of lean meat, tomatoes, and lettuce to whole grain bread for a quick lunch or dinner.

Tip of the SCALE

Always have the "quick and easy" ingredients available. You never know when a change in your schedule may require you to make a quick, healthy meal to stay on track.

Quick and Easy

Crab & Celery

Servings – 1

Time to make – 1-minute

Cost per serving – $1.55

A handful of imitation crab meat and a few pieces of celery provide a quick, protein-packed lunch. Add some fruit and a glass of water.

Good Ol' Egg Whites

Servings – 1

Time to make – 1-minute

Cost per serving – $0.75

A hardboiled egg white and a handful of fruit make an inexpensive, healthy breakfast. Add some veggies and now you have a great lunch.

Tip of the SCALE

"Quick & Easy" meals are great to take with you. A small cooler can hold all the healthy ingredients you need to stay on track when you are away from the convenience of your own home. Perfect for when you're at work or on the road.

Quick and Easy

Chicken & Veggies

Servings – 1

Time to make – 3 minutes

Cost per serving – $2.35

A small portion of pre-cooked chicken and some veggies will make a great lunch or dinner. Remember to add some fruit and a glass of water.

THE BENEFITS OF A HEALTHY MENU

For many people, one of the challenges of losing weight is that they have a hard time eating "diet" foods. Sticking to a menu of bland food items is difficult, which is why I developed a healthy menu that not only helped me to lose weight, but it provided me with time-saving, cost-effective, delicious meal options.

You can now use these recipes to map out your daily menu. Incorporating great tasting foods items into your meal plan will help you to stay on track with your weight-loss goal by allowing you to look forward to your meals, not dread them.

PLANNING YOUR MEALS

"It takes as much energy to wish as it does to plan."

— Eleanor Roosevelt

S top wishing you were in shape and start planning to lose weight. You know the other old adage "failing to plan is planning to fail." When it comes to weight-loss, nothing could be more accurate. Planning your menu is one of the single most critical steps to losing weight.

Even though the majority of people still believe that the best eating habit is "3 square meals a day," most do not regularly schedule and plan their meals to support their weight-loss goals. Some skip breakfast and lunch, while others eat on the run or try to get by on energy drinks and fast food.

Your objective is to keep your metabolism working efficiently during your entire 90-Day Run. The most effective way to do this is to increase the frequency of your meals but decrease your portions. Although some people eat throughout the day, they tend to snack on unhealthy foods. I have seen people eat a donut while drinking a "diet" soda, and I know people who consider a cup of coffee as their breakfast. I was one of them.

I have found that three healthy meals and three "metabolism boosters" will do the trick. to *Control Your Menu*, we must first answer three questions:

1. What do I eat?

2. How much do I eat?
3. When do I eat?

Remember, your body will react to whatever you feed it. If you want to lose weight, *Control Your Menu*. Eat healthy and tasty foods, in the correct portions, at the right times.

WHAT DO I EAT?

The answer to this question is two-fold, as it has much to do with what you DO NOT eat. The first thing I eliminated was soda and replaced it with water. Your body relies on water, lots of it because no other drink compares. Do not fall into the trap of diet soda. It may be lower in calories, but most often it contains very unhealthy high-fructose corn syrup and sodium that packs on more weight.

Sharon P. Fowler, MPH, and colleagues at the University of Texas Health Science Center, San Antonio conducted studies on people who drank soft drinks. Fowler stated, "What didn't surprise us was that total soft drink use was linked to overweight and obesity. What was surprising was when we looked at people only drinking "diet" soft drinks, their risk of obesity was even higher," (WebMD Health News, 2005).

A closer look at their research indicates that the majority of the obesity risk from soft drinks came from diet sodas. Diet sodas are a clever example of creative marketing, with misleading information. If you want to lose weight, stay away from soft drinks, both regular and diet.

FINDING BALANCE

As you plan your meals, you should always try to find a proper balance between protein, carbohydrates, and fats. Some foods, like fish, provide a combination of proteins and fats.

Foods High in Carbohydrates – Potatoes, bread, pasta, oatmeal, apples, bananas, beans.

Foods Low in Carbohydrates – Avocado, celery, carrots, onion, lettuce, strawberries, watermelon, grapefruit

Protein – Chicken, fish, egg whites, crab, cottage cheese, turkey, lean beef, beans

Fats – Salmon, avocado, sesame oil, safflower oil, beans

You may have noticed that beans fall into multiple categories. Beans are an amazing food and are packed with valuable nutrients and are high in fiber and antioxidants. At the top of the list are black beans.

The first step in finding the proper balance in your meals, is planning what foods you will supply to your body. Your menu will include foods that provide nutrients and allow your body to function properly.

Remember, to properly lose weight, minimize foods that are high in carbohydrates. Simple carbohydrates are usually considered to be the "bad" carbohydrates, because many of them, such as cookies and cakes, have been processed and provide little or no nutritional value. Natural simple carbohydrates, such as fruits and veggies, are good to include in your diet, especially if trying to lose weight.

How Much Do I Eat?

Portions, portions, portions! Eating the wrong-size portions probably helped get you into the shape you are in presently. The capacity of the average human stomach is about 1.5 liters. That translates into roughly 6 cups, or 48 ounces. Every time you eat, your stomach signals your brain. As you get full, your brain is signaled that you should stop eating. Unfortunately, most people ignore the "stop" sign in their head and continue to eat.

Your stomach does not stop accepting food; instead, it stretches to accommodate the excess. The bad news: your stomach can stretch itself 2-3 times its intended size. When you have trained your stomach to handle more food than it was designed to hold, you must retrain it to get it back to its correct size. This is one of the major reasons that quick fixes do not work.

To lose weight and keep it off, prepare three healthy meals and enjoy them with a glass of water. Also prepare three metabolism boosters, consisting of ¼ cup of healthy cereal and almonds, or a healthy nutrition bar, and enjoy those with glasses of water.

I like to consume my last booster with a small glass of grapefruit juice, which is a natural fat-burner. It's basic, but it works. I lost weight, kept it off, and fed my body the valuable nutrients it needed. I saw an increase in my strength and stamina while I watched my weight decrease.

During my 90-Day Run, I learned to appreciate the taste of healthy foods. I was rarely hungry after a meal, and if I was, I drank more water. Just stay consistent and you will start to see the difference on your scale and in your mirror. Most importantly, you will begin to feel the difference in your body and mind.

WHEN DO I EAT?

Scheduling three healthy meals and three boosters will be important to keeping your metabolism active. Spreading each of these six meals equally through the day will provide the best results. I eat each meal/booster about 2½ - 3 hours apart.

It is up to you to make sure each meal is healthy, tasty, and packed with valuable nutrients. In essence, you are looking to control the quantity and the quality of your foods. There are hundreds of different combinations of healthy foods you can choose from to make meals you will love, meals that are healthy, and meals that will contribute to your weight loss.

A healthy diet should never feel like you are on a diet. Did I splurge once in a while? Did I fall off of the wagon? I absolutely did, but I always picked myself back up. You are not searching for perfection, just progress. Stay consistent and you will start to experience GREAT results.

Tip of the SCALE   For optimal results, train your body to get on an eating schedule.

Here is what my typical menu looked like:

7:00 am	Breakfast	Cottage cheese, strawberries, water
10:00 am	Booster	¼ cup dry cereal with almonds, water
12:30 pm	Lunch	Chicken veggie soup, watermelon, water
3:00 pm	Booster	½ nutrition bar, water
5:30 pm	Dinner	Cajun salmon, asparagus, pineapple, water
8:00 pm	Booster	¼ cup cereal with almonds, grapefruit juice

This was my eating schedule Monday through Saturday. Sunday was a "free" day. I allowed myself to eat whatever I wanted. But I did not splurge too often because the results I achieved from Monday through Saturday kept me inspired and motivated to eat good, even on my free day.

Successful Meal Planning includes:

- Timing: schedule each of your 6 meals 2 ½ to 3 hours apart
- Breakfast: handful-size portions of protein and fruit
- Lunch and Dinner: handful-size portions of protein, vegetables, and fruit
- Boosters: small portion of fiber-rich foods
- Water: at least 8-10 oz. with each of your 6 meals
- Fat Burner: 4 oz. of grapefruit juice with your evening booster

Pages 107 and 108 show examples of my actual eating plan for the week.

Pages 109 and 110 are templates to be used to plan out your meals for the week.

Here is an example of my eating plan (Monday – Wednesday)

The SCALE Factor: 3-Day Menu		
MONDAY	TUESDAY	WEDNESDAY
BREAKFAST 7:00 am	BREAKFAST 7:00 am	BREAKFAST 7:00 am
2 Egg Whites Strawberries 10 oz. Water	Cottage Cheese Raspberries 10 oz. Water	2 Egg Whites Strawberries 10 oz. Water
BOOSTER 10:00 am	BOOSTER 10:00 am	BOOSTER 10:00 am
½ Nutrition Bar 10 oz. Water	¼ Cup Granola Cereal 10 oz. Water	½ Nutrition Bar 10 oz. Water
LUNCH 12:30 pm	LUNCH 12:30 pm	LUNCH 12:30 pm
Egg White Scramble Apple 10 oz. Water	Chicken Caesar Salad Wrap Fruit Salad 10 oz. Water	Crab Meat & Celery Apple 10 oz. Water
BOOSTER 3:00 pm	BOOSTER 3:00 pm	BOOSTER 3:00 pm
½ Nutrition Bar 10 oz. Water	¼ Cup Granola Cereal 10 oz. Water	½ Nutrition Bar 10 oz. Water
DINNER 5:30 pm	DINNER 5:30 pm	DINNER 5:30 pm
Teriyaki Chicken & Green Beans Pineapple 10 oz. Water	1 Bowl Chicken Veggie Soup Honeydew Melon 10 oz. Water	Turkey Chili Grapes 10 oz. Water
BOOSTER 8:00 pm	BOOSTER 8:00 pm	BOOSTER 8:00 pm
¼ Cup Granola Cereal 4 oz. Grapefruit Juice	¼ Cup Granola Cereal 4 oz. Grapefruit Juice	¼ Cup Granola Cereal 4 oz. Grapefruit Juice

Here is an example of my eating plan (Thursday – Saturday)

The SCALE Factor: 3-Day Menu		
THURSDAY	FRIDAY	SATURDAY
BREAKFAST 7:00 am	BREAKFAST 7:00 am	BREAKFAST 7:00 am
Cottage Cheese 1 Apple 10 oz. Water	2 Egg Whites Strawberries 10 oz. Water	Cottage Cheese Raspberries 10 oz. Water
BOOSTER 10:00 am	BOOSTER 10:00 am	BOOSTER 10:00 am
¼ Cup Granola Cereal 10 oz. Water	½ Nutrition Bar 10 oz. Water	¼ Cup Granola Cereal 10 oz. Water
LUNCH 12:30 pm	LUNCH 12:30 pm	LUNCH 12:30 pm
1 Bowl Chicken Veggie Soup Watermelon 10 oz. Water	Chicken Caesar Salad Wrap Honeydew Melon 10 oz. Water	Turkey Patty Strawberries 10 oz. Water
BOOSTER 3:00 pm	BOOSTER 3:00 pm	BOOSTER 3:00 pm
¼ Cup Granola Cereal 10 oz. Water	½ Nutrition Bar 10 oz. Water	¼ Cup Granola Cereal 10 oz. Water
DINNER 5:30 pm	DINNER 5:30 pm	DINNER 5:30 pm
Salmon & Asparagus Cantaloupe 10 oz. Water	Italian Crab Bake Fruit Salad 10 oz. Water	1 Bowl Chicken Veggie Soup Grapes 10 oz. Water
BOOSTER 8:00 pm	BOOSTER 8:00 pm	BOOSTER 8:00 pm
¼ Cup Granola Cereal 4 oz. Grapefruit Juice	¼ Cup Granola Cereal 4 oz. Grapefruit Juice	¼ Cup Granola Cereal 4 oz. Grapefruit Juice

Schedule each meal about 2 ½ to 3 hours apart.

The SCALE Factor: 3-Day Menu		
MONDAY	TUESDAY	WEDNESDAY
BREAKFAST 7:00 am	BREAKFAST 7:00 am	BREAKFAST 7:00 am
BOOSTER 10:00 am	BOOSTER 10:00 am	BOOSTER 10:00 am
LUNCH 12:30 pm	LUNCH 12:30 pm	LUNCH 12:30 pm
BOOSTER 3:00 pm	BOOSTER 3:00 pm	BOOSTER 3:00 pm
DINNER 5:30 pm	DINNER 5:30 pm	DINNER 5:30 pm
BOOSTER 8:00 pm	BOOSTER 8:00 pm	BOOSTER 8:00 pm

Schedule each meal about 2 ½ to 3 hours apart.

The SCALE Factor: 3-Day Menu		
THURSDAY	FRIDAY	SATURDAY
BREAKFAST 7:00 am	BREAKFAST 7:00 am	BREAKFAST 7:00 am
BOOSTER 10:00 am	BOOSTER 10:00 am	BOOSTER 10:00 am
LUNCH 12:30 pm	LUNCH 12:30 pm	LUNCH 12:30 pm
BOOSTER 3:00 pm	BOOSTER 3:00 pm	BOOSTER 3:00 pm
DINNER 5:30 pm	DINNER 5:30 pm	DINNER 5:30 pm
BOOSTER 8:00 pm	BOOSTER 8:00 pm	BOOSTER 8:00 pm

FACTOR 3 - YOUR BODY

It's not about showing off,
it's about showing up!

— Erik Therwanger

Why is exercise so important? Well, our bodies are made up of more than 600 muscles, which require physical activity to keep them functioning properly. Most jobs today require little to no physical exertion, unlike the farm and factory jobs in decades past. Today, people do not experience exercise as part of their daily routine. If your goal is to lose weight and keep it off, exercise is not an option, it is a necessity.

If a muscle is not used regularly, it will lose mass over time (muscle atrophy). Proper exercise will provide your muscles with the resistance they need to reduce that loss. As early as age 30, we start to notice some reduction of muscle. By age 40, people begin to lose approximately a half pound of muscle each year, which is replaced by body fat. By age 50, most people have lost about 10% of their muscle mass. By age 70, the loss is about 40%.

Loss of muscle mass makes it more difficult to perform basic tasks, like lifting and walking. According to NASA, astronauts who are in excellent shape, experience back pain in space. How is this possible? On Earth, back pain is usually associated with heavy spinal load, caused by gravity. But there is no gravity in space. The lack of gravity does cause a lack of resistance to the muscles. Even physically fit astronauts experience muscle atrophy because of the inability to provide their muscles with resistance.

When you control your body, you will not only help it to shed unwanted pounds, but you will help to prevent the loss of muscle mass. Exercise helps to keep you feeling healthy and looking younger. It is like finding the fountain of youth.

People ask me if they can reach their weight-loss goals by only changing their eating habits. Depending on how much weight you want to lose, you can, and will, lose weight by changing your eating habits and not exercising, but I do not recommend it. You can quickly lose 20 pounds by cutting your leg off, but I do not recommend that either. Do not avoid exercise, embrace it.

Exercising is a critical part in leading a healthy life. Despite all of our medical advances, there is still no cure for the common cold. The best preventive "medicine" is exercise. It boosts your immune system, provides additional energy, and is an unparalleled stress reliever.

Too Little Activity = Too Much Weight

Far too many people significantly cut down the amount of regular exercising they do as they get older. It is estimated that more than 60 percent of adults do not participate in regular physical activity, with 25 percent not active at all. Worse yet, these habits are being transferred to our children. Some 50 percent of children do not engage in the recommended physical activities required to stay healthy. Guidelines in the U.S. and U.K. suggest that children should perform moderate physical activity for at least an hour each day to stay healthy.

Physical inactivity is a devastating, global problem. In fact, Change4Life, a society-wide movement which started in England, claims that "If we carry on as we are, 90 percent of today's children could be overweight or obese by 2050." Chang4Life attributes the rise in obesity to inactivity, especially due to the numerous hours children spend in front of TVs, computers, and video games.

If exercise is so important, why do so many people shy away from it? They do not understand what to do or where to start. **The SCALE Factor** teaches much more than just moving around, it harnesses the power of applying resistance. As human beings, we naturally take the path of least resistance. To lose weight, we need to follow the path of greater resistance.

In addition to helping you lose weight, consistent resistance-based exercising has been linked to improving your health and lowering your risks of illness and death.

EXERCISING REDUCES THE RISK OF DEVELOPING:

- Heart disease
- Diabetes
- High blood pressure
- Various types of cancer
- Feelings of depression and anxiety

EXERCISING HELPS TO BUILD AND MAINTAIN:

- Healthy bones and joints
- Muscle mass
- Physical strength and stamina
- Improved attitude and excitement for life
- Increased brain capacity
- Better looking physique

Exercise is a phenomenal fat burner and a great source of inspiration for my eating habits. I am always less likely to cheat on my healthy menu on the days I exercise. If my thoughts turn to snacking on junk food (and it happens), my willpower is much stronger after I have invested my time that day exercising.

THE PROBLEM WITH EXERCISE PROGRAMS

If you are looking for a way to lose weight by doing nothing, close this book now. The world's "picture-perfect" physiques are not maintained by using only a quick-fix product. Their amazing results are achieved by following a consistent routine.

Exercise programs unintentionally discourage people with the before and after pictures of their "success" stories. Most people do not initially believe they can achieve the look of the rock-hard body in those photos: 6-pack abs, muscular arms, and a perfect butt. Their weight-loss goals are not about appearing on a magazine cover or in a television commercial. They merely want to lose weight to feel healthier, look better, or perhaps, to have more energy to simply enjoy life.

There are a million "quick-fix" exercise programs, routines, and gimmick "solutions" available. I have seen videos claiming that you can get perfect abs in less than one minute per day. I have seen clothing that will "sweat" the weight off of you. And I have even seen battery-powered belts that send electronic signals into your body to stimulate your muscles. These programs have two things in common.

1. They claim that it requires little-to-no effort
2. The person demonstrating the product is in top physical shape

I have met some of these flawless product representatives and discovered how some of these exercise products actually work. During my 90-Day Run to lose weight, I exercised at a fitness club in Los Angeles. I met a guy who was in amazing shape. He followed an intense exercise routine and used cardiovascular training to develop his chiseled physique. He was kind enough to share some of his workout secrets with me and left a lasting impression because of his distinct Austrian accent. No, it was not Arnold Schwarzenegger.

A few weeks later, a client came into the post-production facility I worked at to discuss his idea for an infomercial. It would feature a new piece of exercise equipment, which he had designed. This single bar, which could be bent in the middle, was touted as, "all-you-need" to develop the optimum physique. I tried the bar and it provided some resistance when I bent it, but it seemed too good to be true, especially to enhance your entire body.

To prove that it could develop the promised physique, the inventor brought in someone who had "used" the product to sculpt his body into a work of art. His abs looked like a washboard, his arms were well-defined, and his chest was muscular. Oh, he also had a very distinct Austrian accent. Standing in front of me was that very same guy I had previously met at the gym. I had seen him working out for months and never once did I see him with this "miracle-bar."

Privately he admitted that he never used the bar. He was doing the infomercial just for the money — your money. If it seems too good to be true, it usually is. Stay away from the quick-fixes and start to implement the strategies and techniques in *The SCALE Factor*.

RESISTANCE IS THE KEY

Losing weight is about transforming your body and the greatest way you can do that is to apply resistance to your muscles. Resistance exercises can be performed using your own body weight, lifting free weights, using weight machines, and using cardiovascular equipment. Resistance helps to increase your metabolism, burn calories, build muscle, and provide additional energy.

Our bodies are designed to be active, not stagnant. You do not have to condition yourself to run a marathon, practice to play professional sports, or train to be a U.S. Marine. A consistent, small amount of resistance will help you to accomplish your weight-loss goal.

Introducing our muscles to resistance during our exercise routine forces them to react to the opposition our bodies are experiencing. Many people confuse "moving" their bodies with "exercising" their bodies. In order to get the results we need, our exercise routine must apply resistance to our muscles.

Adding resistance allows you to change movement into results. Your body can easily adapt to an exercise, so it is important to often alter certain components of your routine, so your muscles do not get complacent. Small increases in the amount of weight, the number of repetitions, or the speed of the cardio equipment can help to add the necessary amount of resistance. I have listened to people in the gym boast about doing an hour on the treadmill or walking for miles at a time. Generally, they were just "moving" their bodies on a flat surface, not challenging their muscles with the resistance needed for weight-loss.

Instead, a shorter period of time on the treadmill, with the incline raised and alternating speed adjustments, will create a more effective exercise. You can walk five miles and barely break a sweat but see how long you can walk up a flight of stairs. Being active is good for you, but it rarely helps you to accomplish your weight loss goals.

Exercising with resistance allows you to more effectively lose weight.

Control Your Body with three components:

1. Stretching
2. Cardiovascular exercise
3. Weight training

These are the three simple, time-saving components that I used to lose weight, become healthier, and have a greater life. They will work for you, too.

Tip of the
SCALE   Make time, not excuses, for the exercises.

Questions Before You Start

"To find the exact answer, one must first ask the exact question."

— S. Tobin Webster

Congratulations on incorporating the benefits of exercise in your journey to lose weight. Like most people, you are excited about taking your body in a new direction but probably have some questions. Before you start, I have provided answers to some of the most common questions I have been asked regarding exercise.

IS MY AGE A FACTOR?

Age is only a factor when you allow it to be one. Older adults can benefit dramatically by exercising. It slows down muscle loss, increases flexibility, and reduces the risk of falling.

Parents who exercise not only improve their own health, but they set an example of good health for their children. Children are more likely to exercise, if they see their parents or other family members doing it.

HOW LONG SHOULD I EXERCISE?

Opinions vary as to the length and intensity of exercise. Yes, it is possible to over exert your body. I advise moderation and have designed daily routines to help you work your major muscle groups and increase your stamina with short periods of cardiovascular exercise. You do not need to exercise for long periods of time to accomplish your weight-loss goal. I usually exercise for roughly 30 minutes. That's less than 3% of my day.

WHEN SHOULD I EXERCISE?

There are different theories regarding the best time to exercise. I have found the best time is the time I can stick with consistently. I generally try to exercise in the morning and I am willing to get up earlier to do it. I love the feeling of starting my day off with an invigorating exercise routine. It empowers me to have a productive day and stay on target with my meals.

If I have a commitment early in the morning, I exercise in the evening. Based on your schedule, find a time each day to which you can commit. It does not matter if it is in the morning, afternoon, or evening, as long as it is consistent.

SHOULD I EAT BEFORE EXERCISING?

Eating before, during, or after exercising is controversial. There are plenty of valid arguments on all sides, so I will tell you what works for me. I have my meals at least an hour after I exercise, because I understand that the demands of the body to properly digest food, requires help from muscles and organs.

In turn, muscles and organs require help from blood to provide them with a steady supply of fuel and oxygen. Exercising causes the blood vessels in muscles to expand, resulting in greater blood flow. Blood that would have gone to the stomach to help with proper digestion goes instead to the muscles being worked.

I do not want my muscles and organs to be competing with the same blood supply to do their jobs effectively. I prefer to work out on an empty stomach, but I drink small amounts of water throughout my exercise routine to stay hydrated.

Should I warm up before exercising?

Much of your exercise routine will consist of cardiovascular and weight training. Always warm up before exercising and cool down after. Many people skip these steps because they feel pressed for time. A proper warm up will prevent injury, while the cool-down step will assist recovery. An injury will prevent you from exercising for days, weeks, or longer. An optimum exercise routine for losing weight will include both the warm up and cool down.

Warm Up: Warming up will increase the temperature of the blood as it travels through the muscles. As it rises, the amount of oxygen it can hold decreases. This allows more oxygen to be available to the working muscles, which enhances endurance and performance.

Warming up prepares your muscles, tendons and ligaments for both cardiovascular and weight training. Warm up by doing five minutes on a treadmill or jogging in place. You can also lift light weights, relative to the muscle group you will be exercising, to get the blood pumping. On days I exercise my arms, I warm up by doing a set of light dumbbell curls, usually 10 repetitions.

Cool Downs: Cooling down is critical because it gradually returns the heart rate and breathing to a normal state after exercising. Cooling down allows the body to properly recover, which is critical to achieving results. We will talk more about muscle "recovery" in Chapter 13.

You can cool down by walking 3-5 minutes, or by slowing down your pace while on the cardio equipment.

Do I need to stretch before exercising?

Stretching your muscles is critical to achieving results. It will help to maximize the results of the exercise and helps to prevent injury.

Chapter 11 will provide you with more information on the benefits of stretching and examples to help with your exercise routine.

How often should I exercise?

Research has shown that exercising regularly, at least three times per week, helps keep us healthy. I will share what worked for me to lose weight. At the peak of my training, I exercised 6 times per week for about 32 minutes per day. That equaled 192 minutes each week, which was less than 2% of my week. Can you commit 2% of your time to losing weight and creating a healthier you? I know you can.

Here is what your exercise routine will look like (in minutes).

WEIGHT TRAINING
MONDAY - WEDNESDAY - FRIDAY
(32 minutes)

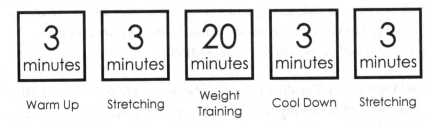

3 minutes	3 minutes	20 minutes	3 minutes	3 minutes
Warm Up	Stretching	Weight Training	Cool Down	Stretching

CARDIOVASCULAR TRAINING
TUESDAY - THURSDAY - SATURDAY
(32 minutes)

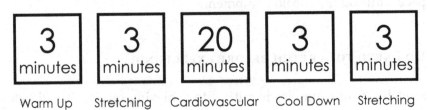

3 minutes	3 minutes	20 minutes	3 minutes	3 minutes
Warm Up	Stretching	Cardiovascular	Cool Down	Stretching

STRETCH YOURSELF – LITERALLY

> "A mind that is stretched by a new experience can never go back to its old dimensions."
>
> — Oliver Wendell Holmes, Jr.

Boot camp started at the crack of dawn with the sound of reveille blaring across the base. In less than one minute, we were out of our bunks, fully dressed, and falling into formation outside of the barracks. We marched to the chow hall in unison, to the tune of our drill instructor's cadence. We finished breakfast and hustled, once again, to stand in formation in front of the chow hall. From there we marched to our next assignment. This entire process took about 20 minutes.

Everything in boot camp happened at a fast pace, but everything happened for a reason. Every physical activity, and there were many, included stretching. Our drill instructors had one goal, and that was to transform us into Marines. That goal was tougher to accomplish if we were injured and sent to sick bay. To eliminate potential physical injuries, we had to warm up and stretch before and after all exercises or activities.

As we get older, our muscles tighten, and the range of motion in our joints can decrease. Day-to-day actions, such as getting dressed or reaching for things, can become more difficult to do. Stretching helps to activate muscles, causing them to lengthen and remain flexible.

Stretching, on a regular basis, is healthy and should be incorporated into your daily schedule.

THE BENEFITS OF STRETCHING:

- Reduces muscle tension
- Improves circulation
- Increases range of movement in the joints
- Increases flexibility
- Improves muscular coordination
- Enhances energy levels
- Improves posture
- Reduces stress

Stretching is a great preventative tool. We could injure ourselves while lifting our children, picking up a box, or walking up a flight of stairs. But the risk of physical injury increases during exercise, if we do not properly prepare our bodies. Stretching is a vital component of losing weight. It enhances our exercises and allows us to properly develop a great physique and maintain a healthy lifestyle.

STRETCHING ENHANCES EXERCISING

Stretching, as part of our exercise routines, also lessens any soreness we may experience. Soreness is a natural part of exercising, especially when the muscles encounter resistance. I love the feeling I get from lifting weights. It reminds me that my body is "under construction." But there is a big difference between being sore and being in pain.

An exercise injury is far different than soreness. In addition to being extremely painful and frustrating, an injury can bring an abrupt halt to your exercise routine and your weight-loss efforts. By properly stretching, you can keep your body in excellent condition while reducing the risk of injury.

Properly stretching your muscles helps you to move them over a greater range of motion. This prevents them from tearing as you apply resistance through cardiovascular and weight-lifting exercises. Properly stretched muscles will be more relaxed during your routine, resulting in less tightness and stiffness after you are finished.

I will share with you what I did to prepare my body for my cardiovascular and weight-lifting exercises. Below are a couple of common questions.

How often should I stretch?

I stretch before, during, and after my exercise routine. Stretching is not warming up. Stretching your muscles should always be done after they have had a chance to warm up. Think of your muscles as rubber bands. Try stretching a cold rubber band and see what happens. Stretching should always be completed after warming up. Increasing blood flow to the muscles will improve flexibility and decrease strain.

How do I stretch?

To receive the benefits of stretching, it must be done correctly. There are many methods of stretching, but they can be broken down into two categories: static (involves no motion) and dynamic (involves motion). My stretching routing combines elements of both static and dynamic stretching, with an added bit of resistance to get my muscles to snap to attention.

Static stretching, the most common form of stretching, gradually lengthens a muscle to its elongated position. Once it is fully elongated, hold it for about 30 seconds.

Dynamic stretching allows you to use controlled movements of your arms, legs, and neck. It allows you to rotate your muscles and increase your range of motion. Dynamic stretching improves the effect of the warm up, so I generally do those stretches before any static stretching.

Adding the element of resistance to your stretching routine allows you to stretch your muscles as you flex them. It is known to provide maximum muscle flexibility.

In fact, at age 41, U.S. Olympian, Dara Torres, won three silver medals at the Beijing Games in 2008. She credits resistance stretching to her success. Stretching is not just for athletes. It is for everyone, regardless of age. In addition to helping to improve your results from exercising, it should be a part of your daily routine.

STRETCHING TIPS:

- **Timing** – A three-minute warm-up session will help to cut down on the possibility of pulled muscles.
- **No Bouncing** – Steady resistance can help prevent tears in your muscles.
- **Breathing** – Do not hold your breath, breathe freely and naturally.
- **Holding** – To safely lengthen the tissues in your muscles, hold your stretches for at least 20-30 seconds; longer if you have a tight muscle.
- **Feeling** – You should feel a warm sensation, but not pain. Stop if you experience pain.

The next two pages feature a variety of stretching exercise, with photos to illustrate the proper form.

STRETCH YOURSELF

Triceps Stretch

Place your right hand behind your head, palm facing your head. With your left hand, grasp your right elbow and pull downward until you feel a stretch in the back of your right arm. Hold for 20-30 seconds; repeat with left arm.

Groin (Adductors) Stretch

Sitting with your back straight, bring the soles of your feet together. Let your knees lower toward the floor. Hold for 20-30 seconds or until muscles feel looser.

Supine Lumbar Rotation

Lie on your back with your knees bent. Keeping your knees together and your shoulders against the floor, roll your knees to one side until you feel a stretch in your back or hip. Hold for 20-30 seconds or until muscles feel looser. Roll your knees to the other side and repeat.

STRETCH YOURSELF

STANDING QUADRICEPS STRETCH

Steady yourself with one hand. With the other, grab outside leg at the ankle, keeping body straight. Gently pull foot up and towards the buttocks until you feel a stretch along the front of thigh. Thigh should be pulled straight back and not drift to the outside. Hold for 20-30 seconds. Repeat with other leg.

BASIC GLUTE STRETCH

Lie on your back. Bend your right knee and lift it halfway to your chest. Grasp behind your knee with both hands and pull your leg toward your chest, keeping your buttocks against the floor. Hold for 20-30 seconds. Repeat with other leg.

SIDE STRETCH

Stand with your feet shoulder width apart. Keeping one arm at your side, raise the other over your head, pointing your hand toward the opposite side.

Keeping both legs straight, bend toward the side of your hanging arm. Hold for 20-30 seconds. Repeat with your other arm.

STRETCH YOURSELF

CAT & CAMEL

Begin on your hands and knees. Round your back by contracting your abdominal muscles and tucking your pelvis. Then allow your back to sag toward the floor as you lift your chest forward. Hold for 20-30 seconds. Perform three to five repetitions.

NECK ROTATION

Start by facing straight forward, with your arms hanging down in front of you. Keep your elbows straight and push your hands against your thighs to keep your shoulders from moving. Turn your neck, moving your chin toward your shoulder. Hold for 20-30 seconds. Turn your head to the other shoulder and repeat.

SHOULDER CIRCLES

Stand with your feet shoulder-width apart. Lift your arms so they are parallel to the ground.

Keeping your arms straight, rotate them in a small circular motion.

Do 10-15 repetitions forward, then 10-15 repetitions backward.

STRETCH YOURSELF

HAMSTRING STRETCH

Sit on the floor with one leg out straight. Extending your arms, reach forward by bending at the waist. Keep your knee straight and hold onto the farthest part of your leg or feet that you can reach. Hold this position for 20-30 seconds. Repeat with other leg.

CALF STRETCH

Face a wall and stand 12 inches away from it. Keeping both feet flat on the floor, extend one leg behind you. Keep your rear knee straight and lean toward the wall as you feel tension in the calf muscle of your extended leg. Hold for 20-30 seconds. Repeat with your other leg.

PEC STRETCH (CHEST)

Standing next to a wall, bend the arm being stretched. Place your hand flat against the wall. Move forward and rotate your body away from your outstretched arm. Hold for 20-30 seconds. Repeat with your other arm.

MOVE WITH A PURPOSE – CARDIOVASCULAR TRAINING

> ## "True life is lived when tiny changes occur."
>
> — Leo Tolstoy

C ardiovascular exercise is one of the most popular ways to stay in shape. But very few people actually achieve the weight loss results they are looking for, despite spending hours of perpetually keeping their bodies in motion. Proper cardiovascular training, combined with weight lifting, will help move you from motion to victory. You will lose weight while gaining strength. You will become healthier while accomplishing your weight loss goal.

Cardiovascular training includes jogging, running, hiking, and cycling. Trainers teach classes on everything from aerobics and boxing to spinning and dancing. Exercise boot camps have become popular in the past few years, promising to get people back in shape quickly. A visit to the original boot camp lets us understand how cardiovascular training works best.

Remember, everything we did in the Marine Corps had a purpose, including our exercises. Your cardiovascular routine must have a purpose too and that purpose is to help you to lose weight. Most people associate cardiovascular training in the Marine Corps as only running. We ran a lot, but to transform our bodies effectively, we added varying levels of resistance training.

To build our endurance, our drill instructors adjusted the speed of our running. We typically started out marching (walking) as a platoon, then after the order was given to "double-time, march," we began to jog together. Our drill instructors called cadence to keep us running in unison. Throughout the run, we would often break into sprints, then back to jogging. If there was anything with an incline in sight, we would run up that path of greater resistance. At the end of the run, we slowed down to marching speed while we cooled off.

By the end of our 90 days in boot camp, we could run for miles at a time. But our goal was to run three miles as fast as possible, with a perfect score of 100 for anyone who completed the task in 18 minutes. When I started boot camp, it took me about 9 minutes to run one mile. By the time I graduated, I completed the same run in about 6 minutes. Because our cardiovascular training included resistance, my body transformed at a faster rate. Our drill instructors did not keep us in motion, they kept us on mission.

You already perform cardiovascular exercises every day — walking, climbing stairs, and running. **The SCALE Factor** will help you to use a simple, time-effective cardiovascular routine which will support your weight-loss goal, and help you achieve a healthier body and a greater life. If I did it, so can you.

BENEFITS OF CARDIOVASCULAR TRAINING

I have found two common misconceptions about cardiovascular exercises. The first is that people expect to accomplish their weight-loss goals by only doing cardio training. Cardio training is effective for weight loss, stamina, and toning. But the best results come when it is performed in conjunction with weight lifting.

The second misconception is that more cardio assures better results. Staying on a treadmill for hours at a time will cause you to lose calories and help prepare you for running long distances, but your body adapts quickly to this type of training, requiring you to run longer distances for additional results.

To accomplish your weight-loss goal, adjusting the speed and incline of your cardio equipment will allow you to achieve greater results in less time. You will also experience other amazing benefits from cardiovascular training.

- **Increased Heart Rate** – our heart is also a muscle. Cardiovascular exercises are great for strengthening your heart and reducing heart disease.
- **Increased Metabolism** – our metabolic rate increases which helps to burn more calories.
- **Decreased Health Risks** – consistently performing cardiovascular exercises can help reduce high blood pressure, manage diabetes, minimize coronary artery disease, and reduce the risk of osteoporosis.
- **Improved Stamina** – develops our cardio respiratory endurance and improves our immune system, which help us to recover faster and avoid illnesses.

Now for the most important question: what is the best cardiovascular exercise? All cardiovascular exercises produce results, so the best exercise for you is the one that helps you to accomplish your goals. I have found that adding multiple intervals of resistance, just like in boot camp, helped me to lose weight faster, regardless of what cardiovascular exercise I was performing.

Because your goal is not to run three miles in 18 minutes, I do not recommend the same cardio training that the Marine Corps uses to train recruits in boot camp. But I do recommend their techniques. So, I created the, *The Cardio Factor*™:

- **Time**   Keep it to 20 minutes or less
- **Speed**   Frequently change speeds
- **Incline**   Alternate your incline level

The Cardio Factor™ worked for me because it prevented me from getting bored and it fit into my busy schedule. I easily applied it to any cardio machine I found in the gym, such as the treadmill, elliptical, and the stationary bike. *The Cardio Factor*™ also works well for outdoor activities such as running, jogging, cycling, etc.

I developed *The Cardio Factor*™ to be a companion to the weight-lifting routine
(Chapter 13).

CARDIO BURNS CALORIES

Everything we do burns calories. We burn calories when we think and when we eat. We burn calories when we walk, mow the lawn, or carry our children. It is challenging to know exactly how much cardiovascular exercise we need for weight loss, because the number of calories we burn will be impacted by our age, weight, menu, and other factors.

One thing is certain, adding resistance increases our ability to burn calories and accomplish our weight loss goals.

Average Calories Burned from Cardiovascular Activity (per hour):

- Washing the dishes: 80 calories per hour
- Ballroom dancing (slow): 125 calories per hour
- Sweeping floors: 185 calories per hour
- Mowing the lawn: 220 calories per hour

Everything we do, from washing dishes to cutting grass requires energy expenditure in the form of calories. Now let's take a look at adding in resistance and see the difference in the number of calories that can be burned by performing cardio exercises.

- Walking 2.0 mph: 95 calories per hour
- Walking 3.0 mph (level): 180 calories per hour
- Walking 3.0 mph (incline): 300 calories per hour (with resistance)
- Jogging on a flat surface: 375 calories per hour
- Running 5.0 mph (level): 435 calories per hour
- Running up stairs (incline): 870 calories per hour (with resistance)

By using *The Cardio Factor*™, I was able to burn as many calories in twenty minutes as most people burn in an hour of jogging. The added resistance helps to prevent muscle loss as your muscles are required to work harder to compensate for the additional incline and intervals.

RAMP UP

Helping people to accomplish their weight-loss goals has opened my eyes to some of the problems with many exercise routines, programs, and classes. They lack a ramping-up period, which allows the body to get used to exercising.

Our drill instructors expected us to be able to run three miles by the end of our 90 days in boot camp, but we initially started with shorter distances to build our stamina. Our first run was less than a mile even though it felt like it was much longer. I experienced a huge sense of accomplishment when we completed it. As the distances increased, so did my sense of accomplishment.

I know from experience that if an exercise program does not allow a ramp-up, you may find yourself frustrated and discouraged because your body cannot keep up with the recommended exercises.

The first three weeks of your new exercise routine will be critical, so we will use this time as your ramping-up period. Even though I had been physically fit for most of my life, I needed to build up my exercise routines over time. This not only helped to prevent me from getting injured, but allowed me to stay focused on my form, breathing techniques, and recovery time.

Half way through my 90-Day Run, I added cardiovascular training to my routine. I purchased a used treadmill and set it up in my garage. Recovery time for my muscles was important, so I always skipped a day in between each cardiovascular training.

Here is a look at the first three weeks of my *Cardio Factor*™ routine.

Week 1			
Tuesday, Thursday, Saturday			
Marching:	1 minute	Speed level 2	Incline level 0
Double-Time:	5 minutes	Speed level 3, 4, 5, 6, 7	Incline level 1
Marching:	1 minute	Speed level 2	Incline level 0

I began my training with seven minutes per day during week one. Everyone should have enough time in their schedule to squeeze that in. For the first minute, I set the treadmill speed to level 2, and the incline was level 0. For the next 5 minutes, I raised the incline to level 1, and raised the speed up one level each minute. For my final minute, I decreased the speed back to level 2 and the incline to level 0.

These seven minutes were harder than I thought it would be but changing my speed each minute actually made the time go by faster.

Week 2			
Tuesday, Thursday, Saturday			
Marching:	1.5 minutes	Speed level 2	Incline level 0
Double-Time:	5 minutes	Speed level 3, 4, 5, 6, 7	Incline level 2
	5 minutes	Speed level 3, 4, 5, 6, 7	Incline level 2
Marching:	1.5 minutes	Speed level 2	Incline level 0

During week two, I stayed on the treadmill for 13 minutes. I increased marching time to 1.5 minutes. For double-time, I again increased my speed every minute, but I did it twice. It looked like this: 3, 4, 5, 6, 7 - 3, 4, 5, 6, 7. I also raised my incline to level 2 and I could feel the difference in the resistance.

I was already starting to feel an increase in my stamina by the end of week 2. The 13 minutes that week was actually easier than the 7 minutes the week before. My body was transforming.

Week 2			
Tuesday, Thursday, Saturday			
Marching:	2 minutes	Speed level 2	Incline level 0
Double-Time:	5 minutes	Speed level 3, 4, 5, 6, 7	Incline level 3
	5 minutes	Speed level 3, 4, 5, 6, 7	Incline level 3
	5 minutes	Speed level 3, 4, 5, 6, 7	Incline level 3
MARCHING:	2 minutes	Speed level 2	Incline level 0

During week three, I stayed on the treadmill for 19 minutes. I increased my marching time to 2 minutes. For double-time, I again increased my speed every minute, but I did it three times at an incline level of 3.

It looked like this: 3, 4, 5, 6, 7 - 3, 4, 5, 6, 7 - 3, 4, 5, 6, 7.

I felt great. It was challenging to get through the third double-time, but I could feel a significant change in my body.

For the first three weeks of my *Cardio Factor*™ training, I invested a total of 120 minutes. That's only 2 hours during a three-week time period. That translated into just 0.4% of my time. During that three week "ramp-up" period, I lost 15 pounds.

As I became more comfortable with my new routine, I added 30 seconds to both of my marching sessions, bringing my total time to 20 minutes. I also began to increase the level of incline, adding further resistance. During my fourth week, I raised it from level 3 to level 4. By the end of my 90-Day Run, I was completing a 20-minute routine at an incline level of 7.

As a result of *The Cardio Factor*™, my exercise routine did not bore me and I felt much better doing everyday activities like playing with my daughter, running with our dog, or simply walking upstairs.

Remember, moving your body is different than exercising your body. Cardiovascular exercises can help you to accomplish just about any fitness goal. But to lose weight, they are more effective when resistance is added.

Cardiovascular exercises enhance the ability of your lungs to expand and use oxygen. It will also increase your heart's ability to pump more blood throughout your body to provide oxygen to your muscles. Cardiovascular training promotes health and well-being.

Bottom line, cardio will help you lose weight. But it is most effective when combined with weight training and a healthy diet.

 It is about increasing the incline and the speed, not increasing the amount of time spent on the machine.

LIFT WEIGHTS TO LOSE WEIGHT

"Strength is not gained overnight; it is cultivated over time."

— David Shaw

Research has shown the significant benefits of training with weights. Although lifting weights can help improve many areas of our lives, for most people, the idea of lifting weights stirs up images of bodybuilders with bulging muscles and veins popping out of their necks.

When I recommend weight training to lose weight, the response typically is, "I don't want to get that big," or "I don't want to get too bulky." Don't worry, you won't. Gaining muscle mass of that size takes hours of training each day, requires lifting heavy weights, and sometimes is enhanced with synthesized assistance, such as steroids.

Weight lifting is a natural part of your everyday life and your muscles are designed to help you lift, push, and pull objects. You lift weights every time you prepare a meal. A small can of veggies can weigh one pound, while a gallon of milk weighs eight pounds. Even picking up a baby requires muscles. An infant can weigh twenty pounds, or more. Weight training will increase your strength and enhance the ability to do your day-to-day activities. When you add resistance, weight lifting will also help you shed unwanted pounds.

Over the past decade, most sports trainers have incorporated weight training into the exercise routines of their athletes. Once reserved for football players and wrestlers, weight training has helped swimmers, dancers, and cyclists. Even golfers have started to use the benefits of weight training to help improve their swing, stamina, and reduce injury.

BENEFITS OF WEIGHT TRAINING:

- Helps to lose weight
- Increases strength and energy
- Improves body-shaping results
- Increases muscle mass
- Improves sleep
- Improves joint functionality
- Increases bone strength
- Enhances immune system
- Boosts self-esteem
- Defends against depression

With all of these benefits, I am surprised more people do not lift weights. I am convinced that they would if they truly understood where to begin. But walking into a weight room can be intimidating, especially if you are new to weight lifting.

In boot camp, we were issued rifles, but we never suspected that they were also a tool for exercising. An unloaded M16A2 assault rifle only weighs 7.8 pounds (8.79 pounds fully loaded). How much weight training could possibly be done with 7.8 pounds? Our drill instructors could think of plenty.

On most days, we used our rifles to exercise. Because these weapons were meant to function as an extension of our bodies, we had to learn to maneuver them as such, and we regularly engaged in Rifle PT (Physical Training) with that 7.8-pound piece of government-issued "exercise equipment."

We held our rifles in front of our bodies as we performed squats and side bends. We kept it raised above our heads while we ran in place. We were instructed to hold it out, in front of our chests, with our arms fully extended, until our arms were burning. We learned just how heavy a 7.8-pound rifle really was as we used it to provide resistance to our bodies. Nothing showed me the significant impact that a small amount of weight can have on the body as that weapon did.

Many people prefer to use either cardiovascular training or weight training. But your efforts are more effective when there is a balance of the two. Lifting weights will allow you to burn fat and build lean muscle tissue. Muscle is a critical component of losing weight because it is metabolically more active than fat. When you increase your muscle mass, you also increase the rate of your metabolism, which allows you to burn more calories throughout the day.

Regular weight training is just as important as cardiovascular exercise for accomplishing your weight loss goal. Like rowing a boat, you will get much farther if you use both oars. There are thousands of books you can read, hundreds of trainers you can hire, and an endless supply of videos you can watch on how to properly lift weights.

With *The Muscle Factor*™, you will be able to duplicate what I did to lose weight. It allows you to get the most effective and efficient results from lifting weights, without lifting too heavy or spending hours in the gym.

Weight lifting can be simple and extremely effective, when it is broken down into its most basic form. Think of weight lifting as a formula: 6 – 2 – 3 – 3.

Here are the basics of an effective weight-lifting routine:

- 6 muscle groups need to be trained
- 2 contractions are required for each muscle
- 3 days per week will be dedicated to training your muscle groups
- 3 muscle groups will be exercised per each training day

It is as simple as that. Everyone's muscles function in the same basic way. Now, let's take a look at how to lift weight to lose weight.

6 Muscle Groups

Weight-lifting programs and trainers often disagree as to what constitutes major muscle groups. Definitions range from three muscle groups: lower, upper, and midsection, to as many as 60.

To consistently lose weight, I identified six key areas of the body which need to be developed. As you get these muscle groups to work together, you will notice increased results.

6 Muscle Groups:

1.	Chest	Pectorals (pecs)
2.	Shoulders	Deltoids (delts), trapezius (traps)
3.	Legs	Quadriceps (quads), hamstring, calves
4.	Back	Latissimus dorsi (Lats)
5.	Arms	Biceps (bis), triceps (tris)
6.	Abdominals	Rectus abdominis (upper/lower abs), obliques (side abs)

Many training programs incorporate too many exercises. People easily feel overwhelmed and ultimately miss out on the benefits of weight lifting. During my first week of weight lifting, I exercised different muscle groups on each of my three training days. By the end of the week, I had only performed eight separate exercises. I gradually increased to three exercises per muscle, finding that any more was not necessary for weight loss.

2 CONTRACTIONS

Every time you lift something you exert force to move the object. Your muscles first shorten, then elongate as you lower the object and return your body to its natural position. There is a common misconception that muscles only grow as you lift (concentric contraction), not as you lower (eccentric contraction). Both of these movements are critical to developing your muscles properly.

A concentric contraction is an action in which the muscles shorten, while generating force. If you hold a weight in your hand while your arm is hanging down, then curl your arm up so your hand moves from that lower position to your chest, you are performing a concentric contraction of your bicep.

An eccentric contraction is the action of elongating the muscle. Here, the tension is due to an opposing force being greater than the force generated by the muscle. The downward movement of the weight in your hand, from your chest, down to your leg, is considered an eccentric contraction of your bicep.

To properly perform both of the movements, you will need to focus on proper form and breathing techniques. Using proper form while lifting weights, will allow you to get the most effective results from your weight training routine. Proper form will prevent you from swaying while lifting the weights, allowing you to accurately target the muscle being worked and helping to avoid injury.

Breathing is a natural function of your body and must be performed while weight training. Never hold your breath while lifting weights. Here is the simple rule to follow: exhale when you exert. Exhale on the concentric contraction, inhale on the eccentric contraction.

If you are performing a bench press, exhale as you push the weight up, inhale as you lower it. In the beginning stages of weight lifting, you may need to consciously think about your breathing technique until it becomes natural.

3 Days Per Week

Most people assume that their muscles grow during their workout, as they are lifting and lowering the weight. Nothing is further from the truth. Muscles actually develop during the rest period following resistance training. A good workout will typically produce some soreness, which is a result of the necessary "damage" caused to the muscle fibers.

Although most soreness goes away after a day or so, research has shown that the evidence of such damage can last for up to five days after the muscle has been exercised. Because growth occurs during the recovery period, I prefer to give each muscle group nearly a full week to do its healing magic.

Often, people try to speed up the results of weight lifting, causing the muscles to exceed their capacity for recovery. "Overtraining" can cause fatigue, reduce strength, and decrease muscle mass, which can also lead to injury.

3 Muscle Groups Per Day

Every exercise book and physical fitness trainer has a slightly different idea about what muscles should be exercised on a particular day. I have seen people train only one muscle per day while others train every muscle on a single day.

With my *Muscle Factor*™ approach, I exercised three muscle groups on each training day in order to lose weight. I developed a routine that would cause each muscle group to work together and allow each one the maximum amount of time to recuperate.

During your three weight lifting days, you will exercise non-competing muscles. For example, I do not exercise my biceps and triceps on the same days, even though both are part of the "arms" muscle group. I also split up exercising the abdominal muscles to different days.

The abdominal muscles consist of upper abdominals, lower abdominals, and side abdominals (obliques). My goal is to isolate each sub-part of that muscle group on different training days. Some "ab" exercises simultaneously train a combination of upper, lower, and side abdominal muscles, so I spread them out over the three training weight lifting days.

- Monday: Chest - Shoulders - Upper Abdominals
- Wednesday: Legs - Arms (triceps) - Lower Abdominals
- Friday: Back - Arms (biceps) - Side Abdominals

SHOCK YOUR MUSCLES

Your muscles have a remarkable ability to adapt to any routine. This process is known as muscle plasticity. Incorporating slight variations into your exercise routine will keep your muscles from getting complacent with your routine. A well-balanced exercise routine will keep your muscles on their toes, so to speak.

A common guideline for weight lifting is the "3 sets, 10 repetitions" technique. For example: performing the bench press exercise three times (sets) by lifting and lowering the weight ten times (reps) for each set.

Alternating the number of repetitions will keep your body from settling into your routine. *The Muscle Factor*™ consists of 2 sets: 1 set of 12 reps, 1 set of 10 reps, slightly increasing the amount of weight on the second set.

To additionally shock your muscles, switch out different exercises. For example, when you train your chest muscles with the bench press exercise, use dumbbells one week and a barbell the next week.

TRAINING MUSCLES

Below is a basic diagram of the muscles you will be training as you lift weights to lose weight.

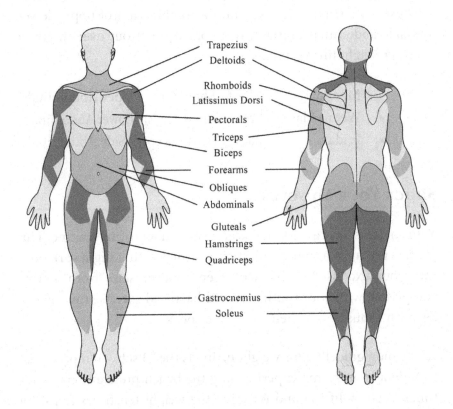

Trapezius
Deltoids
Rhomboids
Latissimus Dorsi
Pectorals
Triceps
Biceps
Forearms
Obliques
Abdominals
Gluteals
Hamstrings
Quadriceps
Gastrocnemius
Soleus

Basic Training

"Accept the challenges so that you can feel the exhilaration of victory."

— General George Patton

Although I started to lose weight by changing my menu, I soon realized that weight training would also help me with my goal. Lifting weights did much more than help me to lose additional weight. It helped me to improve my physique and allowed me to participate in an active lifestyle again.

But I could not accomplish my goal if I "burned-out" and quit exercising. This happens to far too many people because they try to do too much, too fast. *The SCALE Factor* also provides you with a three week "ramp-up" period during your weight training routine.

The first week of your 90-Day Run will require less than 15 minutes for each of your three weight-training days. But it will provide your body with a solid foundation for growth. Weeks two and three will introduce a couple additional weight-lifting exercises.

This three-week period is designed to get your body accustomed to lifting weights and will involve lighter dumbbells. As your strength and stamina increase, you can add heavier dumbbell and barbell exercises to your routine.

Let's take a closer look at the exercises that will help to train all six of your muscle groups. I have included at least three basic exercises for each muscle group, mostly using dumbbells.

The end of this chapter will show you how to put your own personal program together.

CHEST - Bench Press

Using dumbbells helps to isolate the chest muscles as more force is exerted to keep the weight steady.

- PRIMARY: Pectorals
- SECONDARY: Triceps

Start Point

Lie down on a flat bench, with your feet flat on the floor. Keep your hips on the bench.

Hold a dumbbell in each hand, just above your shoulders. Keep your palms facing toward your legs. Slowly press the dumbbells, exhaling as they go up.

Mid-Point

Continue pressing and lock your arms. The dumbbells should be directly above the center of your chest.

Next, lower the dumbbells back to the original position, without resting the weight on your chest. Inhale as you lower the weight. Repeat for the remaining repetitions.

Tip of the SCALE

Keep your head firmly on the bench throughout the entire exercise. Keep your form tight. The dumbbells should not move over your face or your stomach.

CHEST - Incline Bench Press

Considered a compound movement since it hits more than one muscle group, this exercise targets the upper chest area while also working the triceps.

- PRIMARY: Upper Pectorals
- SECONDARY: Triceps

Start Point

Set the incline of the bench to a 45° angle. Place your feet firmly on the floor and grasp dumbbells from the ground.

Rotate them up to the top of your chest, with your palms facing your legs. Lean back on the bench and slowly press the weight up. Exhale as you press up.

Mid-Point

Continue pressing and lock your arms. The dumbbells should be directly above the top of your chest.

Next, lower the dumbbells back to the original position, without resting the weight on your chest. Inhale as you lower the weight down. Repeat for the remaining repetitions.

Tip of the SCALE

Keep the incline to 45°. The higher the incline, the more it works your shoulders.

CHEST - Flys

Flys are great for developing the inner chest muscles. This exercise will give your chest a more complete look.

- PRIMARY: Pectorals
- SECONDARY: Deltoids

Start Point

Sit on the edge of a flat bench. Grasp dumbbells, then lie back. Keep the weights close to the center of your chest, palms facing each other. Exhale as you press both dumbbells up above your chest. Slightly bend your elbows and inhale as you lower each dumbbell to the side of your body, in a circular motion.

Mid-Point

You will feel your muscles stretch as you lower the weights. Stop before going below your chest. Hold for one second.

Exhale as you raise the dumbbells back up, in a circular motion, until your palms are facing each other again. Repeat for the rest of your repetitions.

Tip of the SCALE

Keeping your elbows bent, it should feel like you are hugging a barrel. To prevent overstretching your muscles, do not let the dumbbells go lower than the level of the bench.

SHOULDERS - Standing Press

This exercise targets the inner, outer, and rear deltoid muscles.

- PRIMARY: Deltoids
- SECONDARY: Upper Pectorals, Trapezius

Start Point

Stand with your feet shoulder width apart. Grab a dumbbell in each hand and lift them to your shoulders, palms facing forward.

Exhale as you press the dumbbells above your head.

Mid-Point

Continue pressing until your arms are almost straight. The dumbbells should almost touch. Hold for one second.

Inhale as you lower the dumbbells back to their original position at shoulder height. Repeat for the remaining repetitions.

Tip of the SCALE

Do not let the dumbbells sway back and forth. Keep them in a straight line while pressing and lowering.

SHOULDERS - Side Raises

This exercise focuses on providing definition to your deltoids.

- PRIMARY: Deltoids
- SECONDARY: Forearms

Start Point

Stand with your feet shoulder width apart. Hold the dumbbell in front of your body, with your palms facing each other.

Exhale as you lift dumbbells up in a semicircle until they are level with your shoulders.

Mid-Point

Hold for one second. Inhale as you lower the dumbbells back to their original position. Repeat for the remaining repetitions.

Tip of the SCALE

Keep your palms turned downward as you lift and lower the weight. Do not lean back or forward while performing this exercise.

SHOULDERS - Upright Rows

Great for developing your traps, this exercise can also be performed using a handle attached to a pulley.

- PRIMARY: Trapezius
- SECONDARY: Deltoids

Start Point

Stand with your feet shoulder width apart. Hold the dumbbells in front of your waist, about an inch apart.

Exhale as you lift the weight to the top of your chest.

Mid-Point

Hold for one second. Inhale as you lower the dumbbells to their original position. Repeat for the remaining repetitions.

Tip of the SCALE

Keep your elbows above your hands at all times during the lifting and lowering of the weight.

LEGS - Squats

This is a great exercise to tone your thighs and add strength.

- **PRIMARY:**   Quadriceps, Gluteals
- **SECONDARY:**   Hamstrings

Start Point

Stand with your feet shoulder width apart. Hold the dumbbells to the side of your body with your palms facing your thighs.

Inhale as you bend your legs at the knees and lower yourself down.

Mid-Point

Continue to squat down until your thighs are almost parallel with the floor. Hold for one second.

Next, push yourself back up to the original position. Exhale as you push yourself up.

Repeat for the remaining repetitions.

Tip of the SCALE

Keep your back straight during the entire exercise. Consider using a weight lifting belt for heavier weights.

LEGS - Lunges

Aside from building strength in your legs, this exercise will also help to tone your gluteals and give you a better shaped butt.

- PRIMARY: Quadriceps, Gluteals
- SECONDARY: Hamstrings

Start Point

Stand with your feet a few inches apart. Hold a dumbbell in each hand, at your side with your palms facing your thighs.

Inhale as you step forward with one leg. Bend your front knee and lower yourself until your back knee is a few inches from the floor.

Mid-Point

Hold for one second. Exhale as you push yourself up to the starting position.

Repeat for the remaining repetitions. Then do the same thing for the other leg.

Each leg needs to get two full sets.

Tip of the SCALE

Keep your toes pointed forward during the entire exercise. This will help to keep your balance and correct form.

LEGS - Dumbbell Swing

This is great for isolating the glutes and developing the front of your thighs. It also allows you to build strength and increase range of motion.

- PRIMARY: Gluteals
- SECONDARY: Quadriceps

Start Point

Grasp the dumbbell with 2 hands and hold it in front of your body, while slightly squatting. Start standing and contract your glutes. Use the momentum to swing the dumbbell upward.

Mid-Point

Keeping your form tight, extend your arms fully overhead to an upright position. Hold for one second. Inhale as you slowly lower the weight and squat to the original position.

Repeat for the remaining repetitions.

Tip of the SCALE

Your arms need to act like chains pulling up on the dumbbell.

LEGS - One-Legged Calf Raises

This isolates the calf muscles and allows for greater toning and strengthening.

- PRIMARY: Gastrocnemius
- SECONDARY: Soleus

Start Point

Grasp a dumbbell in one hand and hold at your side. Position toes and balls of feet on a block with your arches and heels off of the block.

Place your free hand on the wall for balance. Slightly lift your other leg by bending at the knee.

Mid-Point

Exhale as you raise your heel by extending your ankle as high as possible. Inhale as you lower your heel below the starting point. Feel the stretch as you fully lower your heel.

Repeat for the remaining repetitions. Continue with opposite leg.

Keep your timing slow and stay in control all the way up and down.

Tip of the SCALE

Keep your timing slow and stay in control all the way up and down.

ARMS (Triceps) - Two-Handed Extension

This exercise is simple but allows both arms to work together to lift the weight and develop the muscles.

- PRIMARY: Triceps
- SECONDARY: Forearms

Start Point

While standing, grab a dumbbell securely with both hands, creating a diamond-shaped grasp. Position the dumbbell above your head, extending your arms with a slight bend in them.

Mid-Point

Keeping your elbows locked, inhale as you lower your forearms behind your head. Avoid touching the dumbbell on the back of your neck. Exhale as you raise the dumbbell overhead by extending your elbows.

Repeat for the remaining repetitions.

Tip of the SCALE Keep your knees slightly bent throughout the exercise.

ARMS (Triceps) - Kickbacks

This exercise helps to tone the back of your arms, sometimes referred to as "bingo arms" because they tend to get flabby when not exercised.

- PRIMARY: Triceps
- SECONDARY: Forearms

Start Point

Place your left foot flat on the floor while placing your right foot slightly behind you. Lean forward and support your upper body with your right hand on the end of the bench.

Grab a dumbbell with your left hand. Keep your upper arm parallel to the floor. Exhale as you press the dumbbell back.

Mid-Point

Continue to press until your arm is straight. Hold for one second.

Next, inhale as you slowly return the dumbbell back to its original position.

Repeat for the remaining repetitions.

Tip of the SCALE

Watch your form in the mirror. This is a great exercise for those triceps but is not a movement you generally perform.

ARMS (Triceps) - Dips

A great way to use your own body weight to burn fat and tone your arms. You can eventually add a small amount of weight to your lap to increase resistance.

- PRIMARY: Triceps
- SECONDARY: Pectorals, Deltoids

Start Point

Stand with your back toward a flat bench. Bend your legs down and place your hands on the side of the bench to support yourself.

Position your feet in front of you, a few inches apart. Keep your elbows firmly against your sides and inhale as you lower your body.

Mid-Point

Continue to lower yourself until your upper arms are parallel with the floor. Hold for one second.

Next, exhale as you use your triceps to straighten your arms back up and return to your original position.

Repeat for the remaining repetitions.

Tip of the SCALE

Do not extend your back too far away from the bench. Do not lower your body too far down. Both of these movements can add stress to your shoulders and minimize the effects to your triceps.

BACK - One-Arm Rows

This exercise highly emphasizes the entire "lat" muscles and the trapezius muscles.

- PRIMARY: Latissimus Dorsi, Trapezius
- SECONDARY: Biceps, Forearms

Start Point

Place your left foot flat on the floor while you kneel on a flat bench with your right leg. Lean forward and support your upper body with your right hand on the end of the bench.

Grab a dumbbell with your left hand and let it hang at arm's length. Exhale as you pull the dumbbell up.

Mid-Point

Continue lifting (rowing) the dumbbell up, keeping your elbow close to your side. As the dumbbell becomes parallel to your upper body, hold for one second.

Next, inhale as you lower the dumbbell to its original position.

Switch hands and repeat for the remaining repetitions.

Tip of the SCALE

Keep your back flat, parallel to the floor during the entire exercise.

BACK - BACK FLYS

Also known as reverse flys, this exercise works the rhomboids, which are found in between your shoulder blades.

- PRIMARY: Rhomboids
- SECONDARY: Deltoids

Start Point

Lie face down on a flat bench. Grasp a dumbbell in each hand and let the weights hang down.

Exhale as you lift the dumbbells up to your sides.

Mid-Point

Keep your elbows slightly bent as you squeeze your shoulder blades together at the top of the motion. Inhale as you lower back to the starting position.

Repeat for the remaining repetitions.

Tip of the SCALE

Lift the dumbbells only until they are at shoulder level.

BACK - Opposite Foot Bend

This is a great exercise for your middle and lower back that forces you to minimize your movements and isolate your lats.

- PRIMARY: Latissimus Dorsi
- SECONDARY: Obliques

Start Point

Grasp a dumbbell in one hand and hold in front of your thigh. Keep your feet shoulder width apart and your knees slightly bent.

Mid-Point

Inhale as you bend and twist at the waist, lowering the dumbbell over your opposite foot.

Exhale as you return to the starting position. Repeat for the remaining repetitions.

Tip of the SCALE

Keep your motion slow and steady. Avoid swinging the dumbbell.

ARMS (Biceps) - Standing Curls

Using dumbbells forces your biceps to work independently and gives you an amazing stretch as you allow for the full range of motion.

- PRIMARY: Biceps
- SECONDARY: Forearms

Start Point

Stand with your feet shoulder width apart. Keep your back straight and your head level. Grasp dumbbells with an underhand grip. Allow them to hang at your sides.

Mid-Point

Keep your elbows close to your sides and exhale as you curl the dumbbells up. Continue curling until the dumbbells are at shoulder level. Hold for one second.

Next, lower the dumbbells to the original position.

Repeat for the remaining repetitions.

Tip of the SCALE

Avoid swinging the dumbbells up with any excess body movement. Let your biceps do the work.

ARMS (Biceps) - Hammer Curls

This exercise is the basic exercise for developing your bicep muscles. You can use a straight bar or an EZ Curl bar.

- PRIMARY: Biceps
- SECONDARY: Forearms

Start Point

Stand with your feet shoulder width apart. Grasp two dumbbells and hold them down at your sides, palms facing in.

Mid-Point

Keep your elbows at your sides and raise one dumbbell until your forearm is vertical and your thumb faces your shoulder. As you lower the dumbbell to the starting position, raise the other dumbbell up.

Repeat for the remaining repetitions.

Tip of the SCALE

Keep your form tight on this exercise. It is easy to start swaying your body during this motion.

ARMS (Biceps) - Concentration Curls

This exercise provides the ultimate restriction of unnecessary movement of your arms, allowing you to further isolate the bicep muscles.

- PRIMARY: Biceps
- SECONDARY: Forearms

Start Point

Sit at the end of a bench with your feet spread more than shoulder width. Grab a dumbbell in one hand and brace your elbow against your knee. Allow your arm to hang straight down.

Place your other hand on your other knee for support. Exhale as you slowly curl the dumbbell up.

Mid-Point

Continue to curl until the dumbbell is at the top of the contraction. Hold for one second and flex the bicep.

Next, inhale as you lower the dumbbell back to the original position.

Tip of the SCALE

Lower the weight slowly during the eccentric contraction to maximize the effect of this exercise.

ABDOMINALS (Upper) - Ab Crunches

This is one of the best exercises for the stomach. Proper form will help you to develop a trimmer tummy.

- PRIMARY: Upper Abdominals
- SECONDARY: n/a

Start Point

Lie on the floor, preferably on a mat, or carpeted surface. Place your feet flat on the floor, shoulder width apart. Keep your knees bent at a 90° angle.

Place your hands to the sides of your head and exhale as you lift your shoulders just a few inches off of the floor.

Mid-Point

Hold for one second and flex your abs.

Next, lower your shoulders back to the original position. Inhale as you lower your shoulders.

Repeat for the remaining repetitions.

Tip of the SCALE

Perform this exercise with slow controlled movements. Do not pull on the back of your head as you lift. Place an imaginary apple between your chin and chest, and keep that space throughout the entire exercise.

ABDOMINALS (Side) - Ab Twists

This is a great exercise for training the hard-to-train muscles on the side of your stomach.

- PRIMARY: Obliques
- SECONDARY: n/a

Start Point

Sit with your feet shoulder width apart. Rest a broom stick or lightweight bar across your upper back and grasp with a wider than shoulder-width grip.

With your palms facing forward, slowly twist your waist, using slow deliberate movements. Exhale as you twist forward.

Mid-Point

Continue twisting until you have reached a 45° angle. Hold for one second.

Next, inhale as you slowly twist back to the original position.

Repeat for the other side and complete your remaining repetitions.

Tip of the SCALE

Do not twist too fast. This will cause you to minimize the effect on your obliques. Twisting too fast could also cause pulled muscles.

ABDOMINALS (Lower) - Leg Tuck

This is a great exercise for working the lower half of your abdominal muscles.

- PRIMARY: Lower Abdominals
- SECONDARY: n/a

Start Point

Sit on the end of a flat bench and place your hands slightly behind you for support. Extend your legs until they are straight out in front of you.

Lean back slightly and exhale as you raise your knees close to your chest.

Keep your feet together.

Mid-Point

Hold your knees close to your chest for one second.

Next, inhale as you slowly straighten your legs to the original position.

Repeat for the remaining repetitions.

Tip of the SCALE

Do not let your feet touch the floor as you straighten your legs. Keep the tension on your abs.

ABDOMINALS (Side) - Ab Side Bends

This exercise requires little movement but provides great isolation to your obliques.

- PRIMARY: Obliques
- SECONDARY: n/a

Start Point

Stand with your feet shoulder width apart. Allow one hand to hang straight down.

Place your other hand behind your back. Inhale as you bend laterally.

Mid-Point

Continue bending to one side until you are at a 45° angle. Hold for one second.

Next, exhale as you raise your body to the starting position.

Repeat for the remaining repetitions.

Tip of the
SCALE

As your body gets accustomed to this exercise, you can hold a small dumbbell in one hand to increase the resistance.

TAKING SMALL STEPS TOWARD
A BIG GOAL – SUMMARY

At first, weight training may seem a bit daunting. But your body will soon adjust to these exercises and you will start to experience greater results with your weight loss goal.

As your strength and stamina increases, you will be able to add additional dumbbell exercises and barbell exercises to your routine.

Pages 174 and 175 show the actual routine I used to help lose 42 pounds in 90 days. Page 174 features my first three weeks, my "ramp-up" period. During these three weeks, I performed two sets of each exercise: 12 reps, then 10 reps with the higher weight. I maintained the same weight during this three-week period.

For my abs, I did two sets: the same amount of reps both times. I also maintained the same incline level for my cardiovascular exercises, but gradually added more minutes each week.

Page 175 features my second three weeks. During this time period, I gradually increased the amount of weight I was lifting for each exercise. I also reached the 20-minute mark for my cardiovascular exercises, but I increased the incline each week.

By the end of week 6, I was dedicating approximately 30 minutes each day to exercising. After week 8, I began to add additional exercises, using dumbbells and barbells.

Page 176 provides a blank template for your own program. Use the first three weeks to ramp up. Choose exercises you like for each muscle group, starting off with small steps. Use this time to focus on your form and breathing.

Most importantly, enjoy this entire process as you begin to transform your body and enhance your life.

My Exercise Plan - first 3 weeks

Warm Up and Stretch: 3-5 minutes before exercising. Cool Down and Stretch: 3-5 minutes after exercising.

The SCALE Factor: 3-Week Planner					
WEEK 1		**WEEK 2**		**WEEK 3**	
MONDAY		**MONDAY**		**MONDAY**	
CHEST/SHOULDERS/ABS	#	CHEST/SHOULDERS/ABS	#	CHEST/SHOULDERS/ABS	#
Bench Press	20 – 25	Bench Press	25 – 30	Bench Press	30 – 35
		Incline Press	15 – 20	Incline Press	15 – 20
				Flys	10 – 15
Standing Press	20 – 25	Standing Press	20 – 25	Standing Press	20 – 25
		Side Raises	5 – 10	Side Raises	5 – 10
				Upright Rows	15 – 20
Ab Crunches	2 sets of 10	Ab Crunches	2 sets of 10	Ab Crunches	2 sets of 10
TUESDAY		**TUESDAY**		**TUESDAY**	
CARDIO	TIME	CARDIO	TIME	CARDIO	TIME
Treadmill – Incline 1	7 mins	Treadmill – Incline 2	13 mins	Treadmill – Incline 3	19 mins
WEDNESDAY		**WEDNESDAY**		**WEDNESDAY**	
LEGS/TRICEPS/ABS	#	LEGS/TRICEPS/ABS	#	LEGS/TRICEPS/ABS	#
Dumbbell Squats	10 – 15	Dumbbell Squats	10 – 15	Dumbbell Squats	10 – 15
		Lunges	5 – 10	Lunges	5 – 10
				Leg Extensions	25 – 30
Two-Handed Extensions	10 – 15	Two-Handed Extensions	10 – 15	Two-Handed Extensions	10 – 15
		Kickbacks	5 – 10	Kickbacks	5 – 10
		Dips	2 sets of 10	Dips	2 sets of 10
Ab Leg Raises	2 sets of 10	Ab Leg Raises	2 sets of 10	Ab Leg Raises	2 sets of 10
THURSDAY		**THURSDAY**		**THURSDAY**	
CARDIO	TIME	CARDIO	TIME	CARDIO	TIME
Treadmill – Incline 1	7 mins	Treadmill – Incline 2	13 mins	Treadmill – Incline 3	19 mins
FRIDAY		**FRIDAY**		**FRIDAY**	
BACK/BICEPS/ABS	#	BACK/BICEPS/ABS	#	BACK/BICEPS/ABS	#
One-Arm Rows	15 – 20	One-Arm Rows	15 – 20	One-Arm Rows	15 – 20
		Back Flys	10 – 15	Back Flys	10 – 15
				Opposite Foot Bends	10 – 15
Standing Dumbbell Curls	10 – 15	Standing Dumbbell Curls	10 – 15	Standing Dumbbell Curls	10 – 15
		Hammer Curls	10 – 15	Hammer Curls	10 – 15
				Concentration Curls	5 – 8
Ab Side Bends	2 sets of 10	Ab Side Bends	2 sets of 10	Ab Side Bends	2 sets of 10
SATURDAY		**SATURDAY**		**SATURDAY**	
CARDIO	TIME	CARDIO	TIME	CARDIO	TIME
Treadmill – Incline 1	7 mins	Treadmill – Incline 2	13 mins	Treadmill – Incline 3	19 mins

My Exercise Plan - second 3 weeks

Warm Up and Stretch: 3-5 minutes before exercising. Cool Down and Stretch: 3-5 minutes after exercising.

The SCALE Factor - 3 Week Planner		
WEEK 4	**WEEK 5**	**WEEK 6**
MONDAY	**MONDAY**	**MONDAY**
CHEST/SHOULDERS/ABS #	CHEST/SHOULDERS/ABS #	CHEST/SHOULDERS/ABS #
Bench Press 30 – 35	Bench Press 30 – 35	Bench Press 30 – 35
	Incline Press 20 – 25	Incline Press 20 – 25
		Flys 15 – 20
Standing Press 25 – 30	Standing Press 25 – 30	Standing Press 25 – 30
	Side Raises 8 – 12	Side Raises 8 – 12
		Upright Rows 20 – 25
Ab Crunches 2 sets of 15	Ab Crunches 2 sets of 15	Ab Crunches 2 sets of 15
TUESDAY	**TUESDAY**	**TUESDAY**
CARDIO TIME	CARDIO TIME	CARDIO TIME
Treadmill – Incline 4 20 mins	Treadmill – Incline 4 20 mins	Treadmill – Incline 5 20 mins
WEDNESDAY	**WEDNESDAY**	**WEDNESDAY**
LEGS/TRICEPS/ABS #	LEGS/TRICEPS/ABS #	LEGS/TRICEPS/ABS #
Dumbbell Squats 15 – 20	Dumbbell Squats 15 – 20	Dumbbell Squats 15 – 20
	Lunges 8 – 12	Lunges 8 – 12
		Leg Extensions 35 – 40
Two-Handed Extensions 15 – 20	Two-Handed Extensions 15 – 20	Two-Handed Extensions 15 – 20
	Kickbacks 8 – 12	Kickbacks 8 – 12
	Dips 2 sets of 15	Dips 2 sets of 15
Ab Leg Raises 2 sets of 15	Ab Leg Raises 2 sets of 15	Ab Leg Raises 2 sets of 15
THURSDAY	**THURSDAY**	**THURSDAY**
CARDIO TIME	CARDIO TIME	CARDIO TIME
Treadmill – Incline 4 20 mins	Treadmill – Incline 4 20 mins	Treadmill – Incline 5 20 mins
FRIDAY	**FRIDAY**	**FRIDAY**
BACK/BICEPS/ABS #	BACK/BICEPS/ABS #	BACK/BICEPS/ABS #
One-Arm Rows 20 – 25	One-Arm Rows 20 – 25	One-Arm Rows 20 – 25
	Back Flys 15 – 20	Back Flys 15 – 20
		Opposite Foot Bends 15 – 20
Standing Dumbbell Curls 15 – 20	Standing Dumbbell Curls 15 – 20	Standing Dumbbell Curls 15 – 20
	Hammer Curls 15 – 20	Hammer Curls 15 – 20
		Concentration Curls 8 – 12
Ab Side Bends 2 sets of 15	Ab Side Bends 2 sets of 15	Ab Side Bends 2 sets of 15
SATURDAY	**SATURDAY**	**SATURDAY**
CARDIO TIME	CARDIO TIME	CARDIO TIME
Treadmill – Incline 4 20 mins	Treadmill – Incline 4 20 mins	Treadmill – Incline 5 20 mins

Warm Up and Stretch: 3-5 minutes before exercising. Cool Down and Stretch: 3-5 minutes after exercising. Focus on your form and breathing.

The SCALE Factor: 3-Week Planner		
WEEK	**WEEK**	**WEEK**
MONDAY CHEST/SHOULDERS/ABS #	**MONDAY** CHEST/SHOULDERS/ABS #	**MONDAY** CHEST/SHOULDERS/ABS #
TUESDAY CARDIO TIME	**TUESDAY** CARDIO TIME	**TUESDAY** CARDIO TIME
WEDNESDAY LEGS/TRICEPS/ABS #	**WEDNESDAY** LEGS/TRICEPS/ABS #	**WEDNESDAY** LEGS/TRICEPS/ABS #
THURSDAY CARDIO TIME	**THURSDAY** CARDIO TIME	**THURSDAY** CARDIO TIME
FRIDAY BACK/BICEPS/ABS #	**FRIDAY** BACK/BICEPS/ABS #	**FRIDAY** BACK/BICEPS/ABS #
SATURDAY CARDIO TIME	**SATURDAY** CARDIO TIME	**SATURDAY** CARDIO TIME

A GREAT Future

> "Great works are performed, not by strength, but by perseverance."
>
> — Samuel Johnson

Accomplishing your weight loss goal will be a GREAT achievement. Your journey may not always be easy, but I am more than confident that you will be victorious. As you embark on your 90-Day Run, stay focused on your Big Picture and the real reasons you are striving for a "new" you. Losing weight is important but keeping it off is paramount. Your thoughts will play a vital role over the next 90 days.

In addition to looking and feeling better, your entire life will be enhanced. As you control your **thoughts**, control your **menu**, and control your **body**, you will accomplish much more than just your weight-loss goal. You will take back control of your life.

By achieving your desired health and fitness results, you will become empowered to accomplish other life-changing goals. During my 90-Day Run, I experienced such a significant increase in my energy level and my self-confidence that I started to focus on other important goals.

I not only set the goal of writing a book, but I have now completed four books. I set the goal of increasing my income and was promoted three times during my last job, with my final promotion to the position of vice president. I also set the goal of starting my own business and now I am honored to be in a position to help others to accomplish their goals — every day.

Just setting new goals during my 90-Day Run actually kept me more focused on accomplishing my primary goal: to lose weight.

Are you starting to imagine how great your future will be as you accomplish your weight-loss goal and other important goals in your life? *The SCALE Factor* shows you how to regain control, but not just of your thoughts, your menu, and your body. It provides a way to gain control of your life — every aspect of it.

Right now, I want you to think of three new, life-changing goals. They can be anything from spending more time with family to earning more money; from eliminating debt to going on a dream vacation. Think of the goals that will help to move you closer to your Big Picture. As you begin to accomplish your weight-loss goal, what additional goals will help you to achieve a greater life?

Three additional life-changing goals:

1. _____
2. _____
3. _____

By the end of your 90-Day Run, you will not only lose weight, but you will position yourself to achieve **A GREAT Future**. By setting new goals, and perhaps resetting old goals you had given up on, I know your life will change. It all starts as soon as you begin your weight-loss journey.

There is no doubt that you will enjoy a great life as you accomplish your weight loss goal. And I am certain many new doors will open for you as you position yourself to accomplish other important goals.

INSPIRING OTHERS TO ACCOMPLISH THEIR FITNESS GOALS

The most satisfying part of accomplishing my weight-loss goal was not how I felt in my jeans or how I looked in my mirror. It was not even the numbers I saw between my feet when I stepped back on my scale. It was being able to inspire other people to accomplish their own life-changing weight loss goals.

You, too, have the ability to do much more than just lose weight. Helping others is not only good for the people you are helping, but it also brings with it many benefits for you. When you help others, you become healthier. And this is one of the founding principles of my company. **Think GREAT** is committed to helping others to accomplish goals - no matter what circumstances they face.

But how can the act of helping others be beneficial for you, you ask? The act of helping others actually improves your well-being. It has been long-known that runners experience a phenomenon called "Runner's High." Endorphins are released by the pituitary glands as these athletes are engaged in moderately intense exercise. You can also experience similar effects when you help people.

Our brains release a chemical called dopamine upon receiving something positive, which is why we enjoy receiving rewards. Our brains also release the same chemical when we give a reward. This causes an increase in our energy level and motivation, referred to as a "Helper's High."

In fact, the State Education Agency uses this phenomenon to help increase test scores, by requiring students to participate in service-learning programs. Students who volunteered to help others saw improvement in their grades. Interestingly enough, positive results were recorded even when the students were "forced" to help others.

Harvard University conducted a study on this finding and called it the "Mother Teresa Effect." They tested the Immunoglobulin A levels of 132 students before and after they watched a film about Mother Teresa's charity work. Immunoglobulin A is an antibody that is the body's first line of defense against the common cold, germs and viruses. After watching Mother Teresa help others, the students all experienced increased levels of Immunoglobulin A. The students became healthier just by watching someone else help others.

Regardless of how you define "A GREAT Future", **The SCALE Factor** will help you to get there by providing the tools necessary to accomplish your weight-loss goal during your 90-Day Run.

Focus on your Big Picture, enjoy the rewards of developing the new you, and set new life-changing goals. Most importantly, be the inspiration to others that you are **destined to be.**

ACKNOWLEDGMENTS

MY DEEPEST GRATITUDE

Gina Therwanger - you are more than my wife; you are my friend, my partner, and my greatest supporter. Your belief in me helped me to accomplish my weight loss goal and accomplish my goal of developing this book.

Brandyn Therwanger - as my son, it gives me the greatest sense of gratification to work on this project with you. I appreciate your artistic vision and your ability to create the illustrations for this book.

Duane Koshenina - as a fellow veteran, I deeply thank you for the 20 years of service that you gave to our great nation. As a professional photographer and co-owner of Gamut One Studios, I cannot thank you enough for bringing *The SCALE Factor* to life by capturing the recipe, stretching, and exercise photos. The time, passion, and dedication you put into each photo will help many people to accomplish their life-changing goal of losing weight and gaining a greater life. It is an honor to call you my friend.

Connie Anderson - It has been an absolute pleasure working with you. Your editing skills and amazing insight have allowed me to provide greater clarity to my message. Because of your help, this book will empower more people to accomplish their weight-loss goals.

ABOUT THE AUTHOR

ERIK THERWANGER

Erik Therwanger began his unique career by serving in the U.S. Marine Corps as an air traffic controller. Leadership, honor, and integrity did not end after his four-year tour of duty; they became the foundation of his life, both personally and professionally.

After receiving the news that his wife had been diagnosed with cancer, Erik left his job in the entertainment

industry, became her caregiver and started his new career in sales.

With no formal training, he began selling financial services. Relying on the strategies and techniques he learned as a Marine, he quickly became a top producer, recruiter, and trainer.

Erik returned to the entertainment industry and became the vice president of a media company in Santa Monica, CA. By building leaders, designing their strategic plan, and creating a dynamic sales system, he helped to raise annual sales by over 300%.

Erik's passion for helping others led to the creation of Think GREAT®. He successfully blends his leadership skills, his unparalleled ability to inspire and develop teams, and his wide array of strategic planning and sales experience, to provide practical solutions for individuals and organizations.

The Three Pillars of Business GREATNESS™ brings together the concepts from *The LEADERSHIP Connection, ELEVATE,* and *Dynamic Sales Combustion* to provide business leaders, and their teams, with a shared language of *leading, planning,* and *selling.*

Sharing his personal story and elite strategies, Erik's keynote speeches inspires audiences to strive for new levels of greatness. His interactive and powerful workshops highlight his step–by–step process for increasing results.

Erik delivers a compelling message that leaves a lasting impact in organizations, creating the necessary momentum to develop strong leaders, build visionary teams, and elevate sales results.

As the author of the Think GREAT® Collection, Erik has combined his challenging life experiences with his goal–setting techniques, to provide proven strategies to enhance the lives of others.

As a trainer and speaker for the spouses of armed services personnel, Erik is deeply aware of their challenges and sacrifices. To help support their education goals, Erik founded the *Think GREAT Foundation,* which is dedicated to awarding scholarships to the MilSpouse community. For more information, please visit:

www.ThinkGreatFoundation.org

www.ThinkGreat90.com

Please visit our website for more GREAT tools:

- Erik Therwanger's Keynote Speeches
- Workshops and Seminars
- Online Training Tools and Videos
- Register for the FREE Great Thought of the Week

More life-changing books in

- The LEADERSHIP Connection
- ELEVATE
- Dynamic Sales Combustion
- The GOAL Formula
- G.P.S.: Goal Planning Strategy
- The Seeds of Success for LEADING
- The Seeds of Success for PLANNING
- The Seeds of Success for SELLING

Printed in the United States
by Baker & Taylor

Printed in the United States
By Bookmasters